WHEN MARRIED
Women

Speak...

A COMPILATION OF VICTORIOUS VOICES

TIMEKO WHITAKER
MANAGING EDITOR

WHEN MARRIED *Women Speak*

PUBLISHED BY
Authentic Identity Coaching, LLC
P.O. Box 36131
Indianapolis, IN 46236

www. Authenticinstitute.com
(317)710-9533

Please contact:
Authentic Identity Coaching, LLC
For Quantity Discounts

2018 Timeko Whitaker
ISBN: 978-0-9863401-6-1
Library of Congress Number: 2018905291
Printed in the United States of America

Book Layout by: nVision International
Cover Design by: LPW Designs
Editing by: ASAP Writing / Dee Dee Cooper

TABLE OF CONTENTS

Managing Editor

Introduction

About The Managing Editor
Timeko Whitaker

Timeko L. Whitaker, Founder and CEO of Authentic Identity Coaching, LLC is the wife of Eric Whitaker and the mother of Daelin and Eyuana Whitaker. She is a gifted Life Coach and International Speaker who challenges all to live an authentic life on purpose. Timeko holds a Bachelor's Degree in Human Resource Management and a Master's Degree in Theology.

Timeko is a certified Human Behavior Consultant (specializing in DISC) and a certified Life Coach through Christian Coach Institute. Her coaching sessions are life changing and impact attendees of all demographical backgrounds while her "5D Authentically Me" empowerment seminars continue to empower clients both locally and internationally.

Timeko is a certified John Maxwell Team Member, Speaker, Trainer and Coach equipped to develop and train worldwide leaders. Timeko is a published author as well as the Managing Editor and Publisher of 8 book collaborations consisting of over 90 first time authors.

Formally a TBN network host, Timeko now enjoys hosting the Authentic Living w/Coach T show where she empower, encourages and equips her audience.

In 2015 Timeko and her husband Eric launched Authentic Identity Institute where they train and certify 5D Life Coaches and Human Behavior Consultants. Timeko's goal is to help everyone she encounters embrace their authenticity and significance. Through speaking, training and coaching she motivates all to reach higher heights, embrace values and achieve their dreams.

With over twenty years of military service, culminating in her retirement in 2008, coupled with ten years of Pastoral service; Timeko has committed her life to serving God through serving others and has dedicated her business to helping all discover the power of authenticity.

Authentic Identity Coaching, LLC
P.O. Box 36131
Indianapolis, IN 46236
(317) 710-9533
authenticidentity@gmail.com
www.authenticinstitute.com
www.johnmaxwellgroup.com/timekowhitaker

$\mathcal{I}$ntroduction

"A successful marriage requires falling in love many times, always with the same person." ~ Mignon McLaughlin

Marriage is God's idea. It was His plan from the beginning. In a me-driven world, the concept of an other-centered union is difficult to grasp and can be even harder to live out. A solid marriage is a loyal partnership and mirrors the covenant relationship God has with mankind. Marriage is the foundation for the family—therefore, for society—and is about so much more than falling in love and living happily ever after. Marriage is the flesh-and-blood expression of an eternal, spiritual reality. Submitted to God, the union between a man and a woman is one of the most powerful, beautiful things on earth. The power of agreement between a husband and wife is a force multiplier in every situation.

One of my mentors is a woman by the name of Dr. Clarice Fluitt. She is a tiny little thing, petite and powerful. At 78 she is one of the most beautiful women I know. I have never seen her without her hair done, her nails done, her make-up on, and an outfit chosen that is just perfect for the occasion. She has more energy than most women half her age. She travels the globe speaking to audiences large and small, is a master executive coach, personal life advisor, and an anointed preacher to boot. Her outlook on life is to always agree with God and I have never heard a word fall from her lips that was not positive, filled with the wisdom of God's Word, and able to be applied practically. Right now as I write, I can hear her sweet Louisana drawl and see her smile big with her eyes twinkling as she says, "God is not obligated to bless anything He has not built."

What do I mean by that?

Sometimes we rush into things that are not the plan of God. Sometimes we take a new job, start a business or ministry … or even choose a spouse … without really being aligned with the plans and purposes of God. Then after we have made up our own minds about what we want to do, we pray some sort of blanket prayer over it and ask God to bless it and make it prosper.

He is under no obligation to do so.

True, God causes ALL things to work together for good for those who love Him and are called according to His purpose (Romans 8:28). There is nothing we can get ourselves into that He cannot work through, bring us through, cause us to grow as a result, and bring it to a conclusion that does indeed work for our good. However, He does not always provide divine intervention to hold things together we had no business putting together in the first place.

Some marriages fall apart. In fact, some were never meant to be entered into. Some marriages break up because one or more parties are not willing to allow God to work in them to bring change. Some marriages need to dissolve because of abuse or manipulation or a lack of boundaries with a dysfunctional extended family. Whatever the reason, I am so grateful that the grace and mercy of God allows these broken unions to come to a place of healing so the parties involved can find peace with Him and have the opportunity to step into a better future. Like any other kind of failure we experience, divorce isn't the end of a story. It doesn't disqualify someone from future happiness or keep them from being able to enter into a godly covenant in the future. Only the love of God can wrap up each life and allow such a promise of hope. Only His grace can take broken people and make them whole again.

No covenant is meant to be entered into lightly. Covenant is a powerful thing and God takes it seriously. When we enter into the covenant relationship of marriage, we need to do this with intentionality. We need to understand the big picture, look down the long road, and know what it means when we say, "What God had joined together let no man put asunder."

What God has joined together ...

When physical attraction or personal happiness are the main goals behind entering into marriage, things will quickly fall apart when the storms of life (or even just the "daily-ness" of life) come to bear. If having your own emotional or financial needs met are the chief goal for choosing a spouse, it will be easy to find fault, become dissatisfied, and walk away when happiness or personal satisfaction wanes.

However, if you enter into covenant relationship with your spouse to glorify God, then your commitment to a higher purpose will hold you when things get rough. When your marriage relationship reveals Jesus, it will model the love of God and become so intertwined with the Holy Spirit that divorce makes no sense.

You may be reading this book because you are about to get married for the first time. You might be reading it because your marriage is in trouble and you don't know what to do to get it back on track. You may have already experienced one or more divorces. I don't know your situation or what has brought you to where you are. I know that God hates divorce … I also know that He loves you. The covenant of marriage is near to His heart. The union of two people to become one flesh is part of His design. He created male and female and blessed them to be fruitful and multiply, to fill the earth and subdue it, and to have dominion over it (Genesis 1:28). Whatever your relationship story, however you are coming into connection with these pages, know that God wants to walk beside you.

Whether you are at the beginning of your marriage journey or starting over with a new one, God wants to be part of your union. If you are in the pain of separation or dealing with the trauma of divorce, He wants to see you healed and made whole. If you are seeking to work through some hard things and save a marriage on the rocks, He wants you to find peace and access His wisdom and strategy for emerging from the valley of the shadow and being led once again to green pastures beside still waters.

I have been married for twenty-nine years at the time I write this. I have the happy privilege of coming from a home where my parents, grandparents, and great grandparents all walked with the Lord and stayed together in holy matrimony until death parted them (my parents are still living and will soon celebrate their fifty-fourth wedding anniversary).

My husband's background looks quite different. He came from a broken home, twice broken to be exact. He had a father in the home, and then a step-father, and then no father. At a time in history when divorce was a rare exception, his grandparents got divorced—twice. He did not have a godly example to follow. He endured abuse by his natural father and witnessed abuse to his mother. He came into our union with no model for what a healthy, happy marriage relationship should look like … but God has blessed our union and he is a wonderful husband and father.

I believe in marriage. I believe it is God's design for us to walk in this powerful alliance and have our relationships with each other grow deeper and stronger by the year. Mine hasn't been without its challenges. There was a long, hard season where vows held me to a promise that circumstances did not reflect. During that time I am grateful I had wise counsel to complain only in prayer and speak to my husband as though he was already the man I knew God had called him to be. I didn't do this always, but I did it often and made it my standard. Instead of hashing out my marriage problems with girlfriends, I took them to the Lord in prayer and shared them only with a small circle of trusted advisors who would walk beside me in prayer, hold me to the counsel of God's Word, and cover me in the day of battle. I learned to stand on the promises of God and believed I would see His goodness in the land of the living (Psalm 27:13)!

During those years, I too needed some re-shaping. I had to own up to my own hurts, my own selfishness, and acknowledge that I sometimes responded with passive aggressive behavior that was anything but godly. I stayed tied to the horns of the altar and let God move in my heart. I worked on my own personal growth and development, and trusted my husband to the Lord—His to adjust, not mine.

I can honestly say that today my husband is my best friend. He is walking brilliantly in his calling. He has stepped into the fullness of the man I was first attracted to and fell in love with. I have grown more into who God has called me to be also. I love him more today than at any other time in our history together—and that is saying something! God joined us. God kept us joined. We have the victory.

When Married Women Speak is a compilation of stories, testimonies, and advice from women who want to see you have the victory too. In these pages you will laugh, you will cry, and you will be blessed and encouraged in your own journey. There is healing, hope, and happiness ahead for you.

Wendy K. Walters
www.wendywalters.com

Author of:
Intentionality - Live on Purpose
Marketing Your Mind - Turning Your Ideals Into Marketable Media
Selling Without Sleaze- Marketing With a Conscience

 *Beatrice D. Beverly* – who is she and how did she become who she is today? What made her want to work with families, mentor teens and women? She is a woman that believes that we go through several phases in our lifetime that make us who we are. She also believes that we wear many masks throughout our lifetime but the key is recognizing our inner SELF and not losing that transparency. Being "truthfully transparent" isn't easy and there is a big difference from being transparent to being "truthfully transparent" and this is why she has chosen to be a blessing to teen girls and women so that they can become independently healthy so that SELF improvement and SELF worthiness can prosper.

A native of Indianapolis, she graduated from John Marshall High School started her undergrad studies at Northeastern Oklahoma A & M College, graduating from Indiana Wesleyan University with a Bachelor of Science (Information Technology Systems).

She has been married to Mr. Anthony Beverly for 10 years and they have four sons (David, Timothy, Jaymison, Tyler and Tia). She enjoys spending time with her husband and sons above all other things.

After working 21 years in corporate America, in the Information Technology field, she decided in 2010 to leave Eli Lilly and Company and launch Genesys Solutions, LLC and work fulltime in the organization her husband started in 2007 (Stop The Violence Indianapolis, Inc). In addition, she is a Senior Consultant for the State of Indiana.

During her career she has won numerous awards. She is a certified Consultant Pair®, Certified Six Sigma Black Belt and a graduate under the United Way Leadership Development program and currently serves on the Board of Directors for NAMI Greater Indianapolis and PYOCA Camp and Retreat Center. She is also CICF Ambassador.

When Me, MySELF & I Turn Into US

Where did it begin? Growing up in my parent's home, dating, married, divorced, dating again or then re-married? What do I say to you that you have not already heard? Your mother, grandmother, First Ladies, mother of the mother's board at the church house, neighbor, aunts, mentors and the list goes on-and-on. What advice could I possibly give to you, well the answer is I cannot; I can only share with you what lessons I have learned and what pitfalls I have had to overcome.

Therefore, if you are looking for that "magic pill" or the "one size fits all" this chapter may not be for you; however, if you are looking for ownership, accountability, and individual growth read on because once you conquer those areas of yourSELF, the relationship will truly be all that GOD would have it to be.

With that said, I choose to start with divorce (a.k.a D)! NOW, let me say that I am not going to go into what happened with that but I do need to talk a little bit about who I became after the divorce so you can understand the whys and why nots of the now.

You see, after the "D" word I became a more driven, independent, venerable, and less trusting woman (better known as DIVT). Not only did I become all of those things, but I also doubted mySELF as a woman - my SELF-esteem and Self-worth hit pit bottom! I became depressed, withdrawn, and very guarded; however, the outside world never saw that part of me, not even my family.

You see I was a black, educated, degreed, strong woman with a career (not a job) making six figures! I wore a mask and I wore it quite well. I was not going to let the world, family, work, man, and definitely not other women see that I was broken and vulnerable and that I had failed at this thing called marriage because me, mySELF, and I never failed at anything.

Over time, I eventually became comfortable with the fact that I was now part of a statistical society that looked at people "like me" in another light. So, you see when you combine all that luggage, on top of just living, I never thought I would be "remarried" because in my head, I had been there and rode that horse and to be honest it was not that comfortable the first time around.

As time went on I picked up the pieces to this thing called life and started on a new path that was all about me, mySELF, and I. When I say it was ALL about me, it truly was! I resorted to transforming our everyday lives into a new norm so that my children and I could function. Being "re-married" was not part of the plan. I begin to "date" – now keep in mind that in my head when you had children and was a divorcee you did not really "date" because your priorities and responsibilities shift. I mingled (a.k.a had "fun") and lived, mingled some more, and lived. Then like a ton of BRICKS Mr. comes back into my life!

You see, Mr. and I dated when we were in our tweens; however, I thought this second time around we would mingle and live, mingle and live, but Mr. had another plan. I remember when he said to me, you are going to be my wife! My response was "NOPE, been there did that" and I meant it. I had my children, house, career, and I was happy with ME...MYSELF and I! In my head I just didn't want to have to deal with the drama that came with a blended family, step this and step that, or the it's mines and that's yours and how do we come together. I did not want to become more vulnerable than I already was, nor did I want to have to be transparent and show someone my scars from riding on that previous horse. I did not want to become a "angry" DIVT again! I did not want him to know that fear was a factor and it played a huge part in my life; however, God had a different plan for me.

As time went on he meets my children and I meet his and we begin to do more activities together. What was different for me was that during this time, he had more respect for GOD than he had for me. I was in awe over this because I had never seen this before. He feared him and honored him, which meant that God was first in everything that he did, said, or behaved. He was not going to risk his or my salvation, nor did he do anything to dishonor what a man should be and was as it pertained to what the children saw or heard. YES, I was hooked, and he proposed at church in front of everyone – I was TOTALLY shocked and caught off guard. We were married, and this is where the me, mySELF, and I begin on a new journey.

We moved out of the honeymoon stage and hence the "real" adult conversations begin. Now, we did talk about things prior to marriage and we went to marriage counseling with our Pastor; however, when I tell you that the "real" conversations happen after you say I do…they really do. Everything from schools, parenting styles, finances, bank accounts, what am I called, what is he called, living arrangements, homes, apartments, chores, housework, drop-offs, pick-ups, oh my goodness the list goes on and on and on – you get the point.

It definitely became overwhelming and I had two choices, work through it or work through it because of two things: 1. I truly loved this man and 2. I was NOT going to fail at this thing called marriage again.

As women many times we jump to a decision before we understand the choices that brought us to that point in the first place. The choices we make have a profound impact on the decisions we make. Some are positive and some negative. Once I begin to evaluate my choices and mySELF, that's when things begin to change to include the "us" factor.

When Your Drive Creates Exclusion

That "D" had a profound impact on my marriage in the beginning, more than I could have imagined as I look back. I was so driven on making sure I wore my mask and stayed on task that I did not realize that I was inadvertently shutting out my husband. I believed as long as I continued to be driven I was doing and proving to the world and him that I was not a failure at this thing called marriage. I focused so much on not being a failure that I was actually failing holistically at being his wife. I believed that if I just pressed on without including him in things that mattered most to me then everything would be fine – right? Wrong! All I was doing was shutting him out of the life I had created for me and my children. I only allowed him to be a part of it if I thought I wasn't going to get hurt or exposed for my truths.

> *Forgiveness is something we all too often say but we don't really do it*

Me allowing him to be a part of it meant I had to give up something that I was still not ready to let go of, the ability to truly forgive and let go of my past. Forgiveness is something we all too often say but we don't really do it (at least I hadn't). Once I understood that forgiveness was an action that is when I begin to shed the burdens of wearing the mask. I realized I didn't have to be driven to the point of brokenness because I had someone there who cared about "us" as a whole.

When you do not give your husband an opportunity to be part of what hurts you, he can't support and encourage you. You will always be driven towards the wrong task(s), no matter what your intentions may be. GOD has given us a clear direction on what forgiveness is and what the marriage structure should be. I was my own worst enemy, so I begin to drive in a direction that built my house into a home for the two of "us".

That I Is So Overrated

Let's talk about that "I". Yep, independent woman and nope, I did not need a man to help me in that space, even after I said I do. When I was growing up my father controlled/ruled everything in our home. It kind of reminded me of the lion in the Lion King; however, my father was a black man and very old school which means a lot of different things for a black family. Growing up in that household made me realize a long time ago that I would always be independent and not have to rely on a man or anyone else for that matter, to do or take care of me. Having this mindset made me very stubborn, headstrong, and sometimes outright rude and hateful. My husband tolerated it because he loved me (babe I'm sorry). Independence does not equate to any of those things.

I realized that my need to be independent came from fear. To me, independence was equivalent to fear, fear of failure, fear of doubt, fear of worthiness, fear of trusting, fear of LOVE! When I finally woke up and realized that being independent was ingrained early in my childhood, I begin to pray for GOD to release that spirit and create in me a new spirit that aligned with his word. GOD did not design us to be independent women, he designed us to be an empathic and compassionate prayer warrior. My husband deserved and relied on my verbal and non-verbal support and all those above attributes were slowing killing "us".

STOP with the "I am an independent woman and I can do this mySELF" attitude because guess what, you will be doing it by yourSELF. Start believing and speaking into existence that "I am a woman that is dependent on my husband to lead and guide me, to pray and support me, to love me till death do "us" part." If and when you are true to yourSELF, you recognize (before it is too late) that you have been dragging around luggage, that should have been unpacked a long time ago. I heard someone say that my FEAR is now faults, exposed and refocused (author unknown)!

V Has Many Meanings

If "V" had stood for victory and virtuous in the first few years of my marriage I would not have scars; however, because it stood for very vulnerable, I was on an emotional rollercoaster that had me questioning everything that he said or did. It turned into a he said-she said, and because he was listening, and I was not, we never agreed but settled on silence (at least I did). I didn't like that feeling so I resorted to silence as it pertained to conversations around the "us" topic, or the parenting topic, or the finances topic or any topic for that matter.

Now, when I tell you that silence is a silent killer it is because it allows you to make up scenarios in your head that aren't true instead of doing the work it would take to resolve the situation. I didn't want to look at my choices; I didn't want to be transparent because this would open me up to being vulnerable which was a place I was definitely not comfortable with. I wanted to continue silently blaming him for my vulnerability, the unresolved stuff and most of all the silence! He was definitely the blame for EVERYTHNG; at least that was what I told mySELF.

Let me ask you, when you plant lettuce, if it does not grow will you blame the lettuce? No, you look for reasons it is not doing well. It may need fertilizer, or more water, or less sun. You never blame the lettuce. Yet, if I had problems with my husband, I blamed him because it couldn't be me, mySELF, or I. But what if, just what if, I learned how to take care of "us?' We would grow and blossom like the lettuce.

I discovered that silence has no positive effect at all, nor does silently blaming him for everything. I had to understand and show that I understood that love conquered and removed my fear of vulnerability. I had to be willing to have the conversation and expose my vulnerability so that growth could unfold within our marriage. Yes, sometimes we still don't agree and there are times when tough conversations have to be had, but vulnerability is no longer part of "us". We are growing stronger and transforming – thank you honey for your patience!

Trust Exposes Truths·

This was the biggie. That "T" could have been a deal breaker and/or broken everything that GOD had put together. I did not realize how toxic this five letter word was until I started writing my "truths".

How do you fully trust when you had already done that and it had proven to harm you to your core? How do you define how much you will trust again; does it come with stipulations, secrets and demands? What word would I have to acknowledge again, that had kept me captured for so long and tried to destroy this union, this love this commitment?

I don't know when I acknowledged to mySELF that I did not fully trust my husband. I just woke up and thought, I don't know if I trust him.

Keep in mind he never did or said anything that caused me to land here. He was/is a GOD fearing, praying man with the most honest and sincere heart I know. He is a servant, always putting others first. He is everything a woman could want, so it wasn't him, it was me, mySELF, and I. I remember praying and praying and all I kept asking for was for GOD to work on me...LORD just work on me. This was my prayer day and night, night and day! I knew it was something that I had not let go of. I didn't want to compromise our "us" and just like that it hit me one day. In order for me to fully trust my husband I had to forgive my past, refocus my drive, release my fears and become vulnerable. I had to forgive my father and my ex-husband so that I could truly reap the benefits of this wonderful man.

This was a lot easier said than done; however, throughout time I discovered that forgiveness was not me just saying the words and it was not for them, it was for me. Forgiveness had to be an action without excuses and yes this was an epiphany that I had earlier, but I had not truly let it GO!

I also realized I had to be trustworthy. I realized I was doing things that made me non-trustworthy in my marriage. I can remember I would go shopping and leave items in the trunk of my car and bring them into the house after he left. Did this action make me trustworthy? Looking back, I believe that my lack of fully trusting him helped me to justify my behavior.

When does your trustworthiness turn into a little white lie? Where did I draw the line? It didn't matter that he didn't know, what mattered was that I knew. I didn't want our marriage to be based on half-truths or questionable trust. Clearly, my action wasn't reflecting what I wanted or what I wanted to give. I begin to understand that omission of information is a lie and that growth only comes from being truthful. I wanted to trust him, I needed him to trust me so that our marriage remained strong and sustainable over time. I needed to forgive so that I could wholeheartedly love him unconditionally.

It was all about me, mySELF, or I in the beginning and until I removed that mindset and understood that I had to work on me individually the "US" couldn't grow and prosper. I had to open the piece of luggage I had been carrying around and actually throw away drive, independence, vulnerability, and distrust. I had to trust with all my heart, become trustworthy, become truthfully transparent and vulnerable, and forgive and refocus on the things that made US stronger. It was not my husband that needed to change over the years, it was me. I asked GOD to work on me so that I turned me, mySELF, and I into "US" and GOD continued to do the rest.

Every day is a lesson that is always better than the previous. Every minute is another opportunity to shine brighter and walk in his light and every second is an opportunity for US to get better!

I will continue to keep pushing and praying with a purpose for US!

I am so glad I realized early that I couldn't conquer what I didn't confront and I couldn't confront what I had not identified. Thank you God for opening my eyes to my D.I.V.T.

This chapter is dedicated to my husband.

Thank you honey for your patience, your prayers but most of all for your love. Thank you for believing in US when I was only focused on me, myself and I.

I love you to pieces and back together again!

Yalonda J. Brown is on a mission to fully identify with her divine purpose by improving the lives of all she touches through her efforts. She desires to lead by example and fervently serve God in a way that He gets the glory in all things.

Yalonda is an avid reader and has always enjoyed all forms of writing since she was a young girl. As the CEO of Just Say It LLC, her goal is to create an impact through public speaking and published works. This is her second book collaboration with the first being, My Story, God's Glory with her chapter titled, Bold, Beautiful and Broken. She enjoys traveling, shopping, and has a creative spirit which she displays in her development of greeting cards dedicated to breast cancer awareness and a zeal for fashion.

As well as being an author, Mrs. Brown is a seasoned professional whose drive and self-determination has resulted in a myriad of accomplishments. She holds a Master of Science in Organizational Leadership and is a certified Development Dimensions International Facilitator. She has many philanthropic interests surrounding her passion for youth development and the empowerment of girls and women. She demonstrates this through her service as a Board Member of AYS, Inc., Pink-4-Ever Inc., and When Women Speak Co. She is also a member of the Indianapolis Section of the National Council of Negro Women.

She is a lifelong resident of Indianapolis, IN where she resides with her husband Vincent and daughter, Kiara.

B.R.O.K.E.N.
Through the Fight of My Life

As I sat in my 4th grade class distracted by the taunting of the bully who was set on fighting me during the lunch hour, I fought back tears. I wondered, do I fight or do I tell? I was a "good girl,", "smart,", "pretty with long hair" as the bully stated time and time again. She told me I thought I was better than everybody and she wanted to fight me. Period. I went to a private Catholic school and we had gone to Mass. I remember praying silently to myself instead of the many recitations that I would prevail in the fight. After all, it was my first fight outside of fights with my cousins. Because I was the oldest, I always felt I won those fights. When the bell rang, a small group of us went to the place where we knew teachers would not see us on the playground. I remember being a respectable opponent and the class was split on who won the fight but the bully never bothered me again.

That was my first fight and I had to fight two other times throughout my school years, in 10th grade and again in college. In both cases, I remember praying that I would prevail in the fight. Fast forward over twenty-five years since that college fight to April 11, 2015, I could have never imagined that the biggest fight of my life would begin when I said, "I Do." I threw out all my preconceived ideas about marriage, and the fight began, not against my husband, but with him. Marriage is not easy. At its best, it's difficult.

>"Dear Lord, make me a respectable opponent
>who will prevail in the fight."

Some may wonder why I would pray to be an opponent in marriage where you are partners; you are one; you are on the same side, not opposing sides. It is a spiritual fight daily to maintain a life and marriage pleasing to God. During premarital counseling, I was faced with self-doubt, self-sabotage, and lack of self-confidence. I wanted to be an "excellent Proverbs 31 wife." In order to achieve this goal, I had to be B.R.O.K.E.N.

Breaking & **R**emoving **O**bstacles with **K**nowledge of God's Word **E**vidence of His Power & **N**ever Ceasing Prayer

"A wife of noble character who can find? She is worth far more than rubies. ¹¹Her husband has full confidence in her and lacks nothing of value. ¹²She brings him good, not harm, all the days of her life."
Prov 31: 10-12 (NIV)

The Breaking

>"God uses broken things. It takes broken soil to produce a crop, broken clouds to give rain, broken grain to give bread, broken bread to give strength. It is the broken alabaster box that gives forth perfume. It is Peter, weeping bitterly, who returns to greater power than ever." Vance Harvey

There were times when I remember praying for a Godly man who would care about my soul and salvation. The breaking came in premarital counseling when my fears came full circle. I remember three sessions that presented me with the most angst; submission, communication, and finances.

"Submit to one another out of reverence for Christ."
Ephesians 5:21 (NIV)

While dating, we both were selfish, self-centered, used to doing things our way, and determined to one up the other. The thought of submitting to the needs of another person for a lifetime scared me. How would we live up to God's expectations in this area? While I loved my husband very much, I felt submitting to his decisions was sometimes difficult. Because of my education and leadership roles in my career, I often felt that my choices and goals were superior to his. It took my husband saying to me one day in one of our discussions that he was not one of the students I worked with and our home is not a boardroom. I was guilty as charged. I also did not take into consideration how this mode of communication could possibly make him feel disrespected and/or threatened his ability to lead our home. There are times when we both fight to assert our independence...or allow our willfulness to supersede submission. I had to repent and allow my husband to lead our home. When I doubted him, I prayed that God would speak to him. But God!

"Death and life [are] in the power of the tongue: and they that love it shall eat the fruit thereof." Proverbs 18:21 (KJV)

Going into marriage, controlling my mouth was a major obstacle for me. Communicating in a Godly way to resolve conflict was often the last thing on my mind. To be reminded that ungodly communication is a heart issue and that the way that I was communicating with my then fiancé was sinful was piercing. We both knew this area would be a key focus for us for the rest our lives. I wanted my words to be pleasing to God and to my husband. I am commanded to lift him up, be loving even in disagreements, and affirm him.

> *I wanted my words to be pleasing to God and to my husband.*

Finance was an area in which my husband had serious concerns. I told him early on when I saw we were getting serious that I had credit issues. I remember us driving from that counseling session not saying much to one another at all. The discussion of marriage being "give and take" and the reminder that money management was often a cause of considerable friction and disharmony in many marriages. I knew I would have to earn his trust. But God! He knew what I needed. He sent me a strong, responsible, financial manager of our home. He sent me someone to partner with me in an area in which I was weak. We are navigating this area and working as a team to figure out what works for us.

The Removing

After years of dating and multiple break-ups, my husband and I made a decision to stop running away from God's plan for us and both committed to seeking a relationship guided by Godly principles. When we started to demonstrate a submission to each other's needs, we became more aware of how God designed our roles as husband and wife. We are sometimes overwhelmed at the blessings that come from following God's marital instructions.

Obstacles to a Godly Marriage

Honestly, 2016 is still somewhat of a blur. We were married in spring of 2015 and I lost my dear maternal Grandmother in the fall of 2015. Work was extremely demanding; a work life balance did not exist for me. Stress was taking a toll on my health yet I kept smiling through life's grind. I was learning to be a wife. I was accustomed to putting everyone's needs before my own. I was spiraling out of control and hiding it well.

What would I do when marriage felt hard or when I didn't feel like fighting to hold my tongue, be respectful, or just overall not want to be bothered? There are days when I simply did not want to cook another meal. There were times when I did not want to be intimate with my husband. The fight includes all areas, including the bedroom.

Though my husband and I experienced a significant period of abstinence prior to marriage, when we first became sexually active, I put so much effort into pleasing him physically and visually. I remember our counseling session on intimacy. I was amazed that God had even designed how sex and intimacy in marriage is expected and intended to be pleasurable and another form of submission to each other. When I thought of all the ungodly scenarios of my past, I was ashamed and convicted that in the most sacred bedroom of all, I was not allowing the Holy Spirit to permeate this area of my marriage.

Sin usually lurks somewhere in the midst of discord. I learned to call it out as sin and a trick of Satan. I chose joy in the midst of life's demands. I chose patience through the process to await the promises God made to me. God has equipped us with all we need in the fruit of the spirit; all we have to do is follow His instruction on how to develop and maintain a Godly marriage by being the women He has called me to be.

When I put my faith and dependency all in Him, He showed up and moved in my life. God knew…He always knew. My testimony is strengthened. God stands on His promises and He was moving in our, mine and my husband's life. God is protecting me and my family. He is giving us great life experiences in the midst of the storms. I am better prepared to grow and bloom as a wife so I may live and love abundantly.

Knowledge of God's Word

What does God say about marriage? What does God command of a Godly Wife? According to author, Martha Peace in the book titled, *The Excellent Wife,* "God's will for every Christian wife is that her most important ministry be to her husband (Genesis 2:18). She goes on to state, "After a wife's own personal relationship with the Lord Jesus Christ, nothing else should have greater priority."

The Bible gives us the road map. There is nothing about marriage that God has not addressed in His word. Marriage was hard because it required us to think and act differently than we had done in any prior relationship. When I dated my husband and even when we were first married, I made a huge effort to study my man. I wanted to know how he thought, what he liked, why he did things. I wanted to please him. I wanted to make it my mission to love him with all I had in me and be the best wife I could be. Galatians 6:5 NIV states, *"For each one should carry their own load."* Since the fall of Adam and Eve, our sinful nature is inherent. We are each responsible for our conduct in the marriage. I found myself blaming my husband when there was a breakdown in our relationship which was wrong. But God!

Evidence of His Power

There were times when I would throw things up in my husband's face that he had stated in counseling that he was not demonstrating to my satisfaction. How dare I not trust God to do what He said he would? I had to check myself. I realized it was not my job to make my husband more holy. That is God's job. I stopped asking my husband to pray with me more, go to church more, or to seek God in the way I wanted him to. As a wife, I have to ensure that I am doing what God commands me to do and He will do the rest.

God has shown Himself faithful to His promises. Our marriage experienced a shift when God used people, situations and breakthroughs to show us it resulted from nothing but His hands, grace and mercy. There is nothing sexier to me than when my husband acknowledges God at work in our lives.

I made a choice to submit my marriage and my life to God. We have found that the closer we are to God, the closer we are to each other. I gained such confidence in knowing that God has given me all I need to come under my husband's and His authority.

Never Ceasing Prayer

Submit all things to God in prayer. I did not understand that marriage would take the term "war room" to another level. As I basked in my newlywed bliss in the year leading up to our first anniversary, I know God deserves all the glory and honor to bring me joy with a man who accepted all of me.

After our first anniversary, it seemed all hell broke loose and I did not see it coming. During that second year, we both struggled. My husband and I loved each other deeply, but we didn't fight well. Increasingly, disagreements seemed to spiral quickly into petty arguments that often ended with days of awkward silence. Before we knew it, one of us was yelling or walking out of the room. Both of us were hurt and frustrated. We always made up, eventually, but the toll was high. Each new fight seemed to escalate faster than the last one, leaving us drained of energy and affection. After nearly two years of marriage, I was worried about all of the negativity that had somehow crept into our life together. We grew further away from the Godly principles we had committed would guide our marriage.

It was during these times that I was reminded that Satan wanted my marriage to fail. He is a vicious opponent without mercy. If I did not fight for my marriage, *he would*. My prayer life changed from prayers based on my fleshly desires to prayers to fulfil God's purpose and will for my life. My husband and I made some essential agreements going into our marriage. Some of those agreements were:

    a.   **To strive for a Godly marriage.** Achieving oneness without God is nearly impossible. Period.

    b.   **Till Death Do Us Part**, unless someone cheats. We agreed infidelity is a non-negotiable.

    c.   **We are in this forever!** Before we were married, the joke was that we both had the potential to be a runaway bride or groom. Our tendency while dating was when things got rough, we broke up. We were ready for the fight (face the good, bad, and ugly) and avoid our flight tendencies (run and/or avoid the work/effort).

    d.   **Have a lot of fun.** My husband and I enjoy being friends and nurturing our need to getaway and do the things we enjoy. This was important to us but when life happens and date nights are fewer and the effort is lagging, we fight to get back to this agreement. We love making each other happy.

    e.   **Make each other a priority.** This was and still is at times an adjustment for us as we both had never been married. He gained an almost adult daughter. We both had been single for a very long time and set in our ways. If you want to grow and progress in any area of your life, you have to focus and put a lot of time and energy into it. If you don't make your marriage a priority, you'll grow apart instead of growing together. By us getting married later in life when many of our closest friends are seasoned married couples, we can only pray that God gives us ample time together to enjoy our lives and continue to create an amazing union.

I believe every marriage is worth fighting for and while some have Biblical reasons for divorce, I still believe God can rescue every marriage-IF- there are two willing people. But if you are married, whatever condition your marriage may be in today, I encourage you to fight for it. Marriage takes work and a solid understanding of God's word. No marriage is perfect, but I am full of joy because I am with my soulmate and I could not imagine life without him and most importantly, God chose us for one another. As a last note, I would like to share a prayer I recite as I continue to fight the good fight.

Dear, Lord, Transform me.

You have promised Vincent that I am a gift from you. I want to be an excellent wife to my husband, one who consistently brings him honor. (Proverbs 18:22, 12:4)

You know every one of my weaknesses and how they are impacting my role as Vincent's helpmate. Lead me, Lord, to recognize the ungodliness hiding in my will, my expectations, and how I express my emotions. I want to surrender them to You for healing. Show me where I am investing my attention in things that will deteriorate my relationship with Vincent. (2 Corinthians 12:9–10; Luke 12:2; 2 Corinthians 4:18; Ephesians 1:8, 17).

Let the power of Your Word transform my motives. Coach me relentlessly to be a wife who respects my husband in word and deed. Cause Your tenderness, gentleness, kindness, and humility to become my own. (Romans 12:2; Ephesians 5:22–24; Colossians 3:12)

I want to be a joyful wife who does not harass my husband with quarrels and fretfulness. Please use me to create a peaceful home for him. Use me to encourage him, bear his burdens, and reflect Your extravagant love for him. (Hebrews 13:5; Philippians 4:11-12; 2 Thessalonians 3:16; 1 Thessalonians 5:11; Galatians 6:2; Ephesians 3:18–19)

Vincent and I are joined together as one. Our desire is for You first, and then for one another. We will forever be satisfied with one another because our love for one another is based on a love for You. I declare that Vincent and I will satisfy one another sexually and intimately. Our marriage bed is sacred. Help us both to reject anyone or anything that attempts to defile that sanctity. (Proverbs 5:18-23; Malachi 2:15; Proverbs 18:10; 1 Corinthians 10:13)

May our souls feast only on You. (Psalm 63:5)

I pray these things with complete confidence in Jesus and Your Spirit at work in our marriage.
Amen.

White, Jennifer O. "5 Powerful Prayers Every Wife Needs to Pray over Her Husband." Bible Study Tools, www.biblestudytools.com/bible-study/explore-the-bible/5-powerful-prayers-every-wife-needs-to-pray-over-her-husband.html.

Kiahna Davis will tell you she is no expert in marriage but has celebrated almost two decades with the best husband this side of heaven. Together, they are an explosive couple who ebb and flow with each other. For example, one loves to do dishes, the other one laundry. One loves to cook, the other one order out. Loving her husband is a daily treat and one of the best things to come from their love for each other is their wonderful daughter Chelsea.

She is the First Lady of Life Community AME Church, where she serves with passion and compassion alongside her husband, Rev. Jerry E. Davis, III, Senior Pastor.

Kiahna also has a passion for helping the people around her see the power inside of them and help produce their awakening. She has started an experience called Sacred and Stunning, a movement created to celebrate, inspire and promote women and womanhood through faith. It seeks to help women embrace their true essence (existence) and create an environment where their God-given purpose can be illustrated and supported.

Kiahna has spent two decades in the manufacturing and banking industries in financial and operational leadership, from staff accountant to Chief Financial Officer. She earned her Bachelor of Science Degree from Indiana University, Bloomington in Finance and her Master of Business Administration in Accounting from Indiana Wesleyan University, Marion. She has served on numerous non-profit boards and a member of many professional and community organizations.

Who Wears the Pants?

When I watch him sleeping, talking, or just thinking, I ask myself what is going on in that mind of his. I know the pressure he has on his shoulders. Heck just being of Nubian heritage and walking out in the neighborhood can be stressful. But this day I looked at him differently. Today I understood my role as his wife, cheerleader, his kingmaker. I had not always looked upon him that way. At times my ambition and desire overshadowed my role as a wife and helpmeet. Not on purpose; I am not apologizing for being a "strong woman." Nonetheless, it took me over ten years of marriage to understand I could be superwoman and submit. Being an executive did not require me to forgo my role as a wife.

It's incredible because I think he always knew. He knew that both existed in me. Even after our first date 20 years ago when I made the proclamation, "I don't want to be married" and "I don't need a man," he saw through that foolishness. Like many of my progressive counterparts, I was raised with a spirit of self-sufficiency; An "I can do it all by myself" attitude. I was brainwashed to believe I could do this all by myself. As the saying goes, I fell for it; hook, line, and sinker. The world was mine because I was of a generation in which access to college, knowledge, and opportunity was more significant than generations past.

Yes, I just knew I did not want to be married. For what? On the one hand, I was determined. Determined to be the best. The best at everything. It did not matter, but I knew a few things: 1) I could take care of myself, 2) I wasn't going to be broke, and 3) I could pamper myself. On the other hand, I had not seen many great marriages in my lifetime. My parents divorced when I was young without a lot of fanfare.

I was ok with being educated, successful, and single. I did not want someone in my life to "mooch" off me. I had worked hard to stay focused, stay out of trouble, and stay away from mediocrity. I did not need a man who was going to drain all my strength.

Just a few months before my first date with my now husband, I was dating a guy who I knew was a bust. He was cute, and I was in a new city starting my new corporate job. It was good to have someone to talk to...some company. But soon I noticed we only went out in my neighborhood (I lived out in the suburbs) and never around his crib. I thought to myself; *he is either trying to hide me or hide something from me.* One thing I was clear about was I was not going to be that chick. I would rather be lonely than to deal with games, wondering if I matter. I watch women I love be the "side chick" holding on to empty promises watching him move on and marry "up" later.

Nope, I was not that chick; he found out the hard way. One day he showed up at my apartment with a suitcase in hand and tried to sweet talk me into allowing him to move in. And he presented it as if I was the one who was lucky he asked. I was like HELL NO! That was the last day I saw him. To this day, I do not know what happened to him. But this situation proved out my theory about men and relationships. No, I just wasn't having all the drama.

I just did not want a needy man. I saw women lining up for needy men throughout my childhood. These were old men who were still in need of a "mama." I knew it was going to be hard enough to take care of myself, and I honestly did not want the burden of taking care of another adult. It was stressful enough just thinking about it.
Then Jerry came along.

When I said "I do" to Jerry, I did so seeing the enormous potential and promise that lay ahead for him. I saw his brilliance and genius. For some it seemed geeky; I saw life with someone who could match my intelligence. And it helped he was kind and a gentleman.

Soon after the wedding and the honeymoon, I wanted to begin this life with what two working professionals could provide. We were young, educated, and God-fearing. We had no children at the time, so our disposable income afforded us the ability to go....travel, eat out, shop, contribute, participate and be a part.

During that time our wings were stretched out and soaring. I had my career roadmap; my husband had pads of paper with vision and ministry ideas. We were moving forward together with a bundle of energy and promise. For me, however, there was still this tension. It was unsaid; if you didn't look close enough, you would miss it.

It was my independence. Or at least the facade of it. Often what we think we want and what we need are two different things. I didn't even realize that in my marriage that old philosophy of "I don't need a man" began to manifest in subtle ways. For years my husband would walk me to the car and open the door. In the beginning, I use to HATE it. Maybe it was because I didn't believe I deserved it. I had NEVER witnessed in real life a man perform such chivalrous acts. Perhaps I assumed that there was a huge price that I would have to pay down the line for such an act of humility. At times I would get tense and almost angry inside because

> *It was my independence. Or at least the facade of it.*

I thought it was a sign of weakness. I am not sure, and perhaps that deserves its own focused reflection, but I do know I would be internally pissed-off.

What started off as a smile and a thank you for opening up my door soon turned into "I'm good" and "no need." I did not care how my husband received that. I never paused to see the effect of such rejection. I did not see the bitterness building in him. I honestly thought I was doing him a favor and the fuss was not necessary.

Over the years, we have had climatic arguments about not understanding each other. One dealt with my lack of desire to make my husband's plate. I won't go into the details but let's say because I wouldn't make it someone else did. Now I am not the jealous type, but this is MY HUSBAND. At that moment I realized that if I don't listen to what my husband's real desires are we might not make it.

So, I began to pray.

I was told to read and meditate on the passage of scripture in Ephesians 5.

Let me just say this, STOP using Ephesians 5 to justify gender roles. For most superwomen like me, you will get nowhere. We will shut down and move on. If you are going to use Ephesians 5, at least use it to do more than justify gender roles. Use it to talk about God's desire for mutual love and respect in the family. I didn't start with Ephesians. I started with Genesis. I figured let me understand the beginning; what God's original intent for Man and Woman, Husband and Wife.

GOD'S PLAN OF SUITABILITY

As I looked over the first chapters of the book of Beginning, I noticed everything was created in pairs. Light didn't exist without darkness. sky and earth were formed. Water co-existed with land, evening and day. Every living thing was created, and God looked back and saw that everything was good.

And God said, *"Let the land produce living creatures according to their kinds: the livestock, the creatures that move along the ground, and the wild animals, each according to its kind." And it was so. God made the wild animals according to their kinds, the livestock according to their kinds, and all the creatures that move along the ground according to their kinds. And God saw that it was good",* (Genesis 1:24-25 NIV).

Initially, when creating man, he only physically created Adam. But soon looked and said that was not suitable.

"The Lord God said, 'It is not good for the man to be alone. I will make a helper suitable for him.' Now the Lord God had formed out of the ground all the wild animals and all the birds in the sky. He brought them to the man to see what he would name them; and whatever the man called each living creature, that was its name. So the man gave names to all the livestock, the birds in the sky and all the wild animals. But for Adam, no suitable helper was found. So the Lord God caused the man to fall into a deep sleep; and while he was sleeping, he took one of the man's ribs and then closed up the place with flesh. Then the Lord God made a woman from the rib he had taken out of the man, and he brought her to the man'", (Genesis 2: 18-22 NIV).

Eve's creation is a story of strength, completion, and almost rescue for Adam. Adam had been given the power to name and oversee every living creature, in his search for something that would complete him, God was not happy allowing Adam to be the only human living in the garden. The solution for completeness was Eve.

For a strong-willed woman like myself that was liberating. To know God's solution for Adam was Eve. In the creation of women, we had the power through our creator to change the way humans would lead and operate on the earth. Without his creation of woman, His plan was not complete.

Now, this is a different story than some of us hear about real submission.

It felt good to understand my purpose, power, and authority co-existed with the first man Adam, and it produces completeness and suitability in God's eye. This experience did not detract from Adam's role of being first. But it solidified my self-identification with Eve who was created to help, produce suitability, and rescue Adam from a possible lonely existence.

TEAMWORK

Teamwork makes the dream work. Whoever coined that phrase was absolutely right. We were all created for different roles on the same team. Like sports teams, marriage is the ultimate team. When everyone is in their proper position, winning is possible. The Chicago Bulls were the team in the 90's. And although there was a lot of hype around Michael Jordan, 'MJ' would never have achieved what he did without a great team. I can still hear Coach Phil Jackson on the sidelines yelling, "Scottie," as in Scottie Pippen. Scottie was the perfect teammate. MJ's magic was in Scottie; he provided what the team needed for others' gifts to blossom on the court. Without Scottie, there would be no MJ. They teamed up to earn six championship rings during their time together between 1989-1996.

That's like marriage. The power of team can catapult a family's success and position. I had to understand that when I position my strength with my husband's power, it did not diminish me. Instead, it completed me. God created a wife to be a complement inside a divinely strong team in Christ. The creation of the union of husband and wife reflects God's complete plan, counterparts reflecting God's FULL IMAGE.

"So God created mankind in his own image, in the image of God he created them; male and female he created them." (Genesis 1:24 NIV).

Together completion is obtained.

MAKING HIS PLATE DOES NOT MAKE YOU LESS POWERFUL

My mother-in-law-to-be hosted an engagement party for Jerry and I a month after he proposed. As I was fixing my plate, one of Jerry's aunts asked me if I was going to prepare his dish. After I told her, "No," she told me, "Don't start what you can't keep up." Suffice to say, I was more than happy to take that advice as starting the practice of fixing Jerry's plate, let alone keeping it up, was the furthest thing from my mind. For me, fixing a man's plate was a symbol of demeaning servitude.

After understanding my power, I was able to embrace my role. The enemy tries to make us believe our husband is the enemy. Confusion enters into an otherwise healthy marriage and relationship. And soon the idea of being of service turns into a concept of slavery, resentment seeps in because we never wanted our power to be marginalized to just making his plate.

Making my husband's plate is neither a requirement to being a good wife nor is it something I resent. It is what it is. Like anything else my husband appreciates as a symbol of honor, I do it willingly with the understanding that lifting him in no way lowers me. In fact, the opposite is true. Like an elevator that lifts hotel guests to the penthouse level, I can't lift my husband without lifting myself at the same time. More than that, it is the power of the elevator, not the power of the guests that allows both the elevator and the guests to reach the penthouse. Whenever I willingly do things that honor my husband, I am not displaying weakness; I am showing power.

The power I display when I choose to make my husband's plate is not power in a vacuum. It is the same power I show when I go to work as an executive. It is the same power I display when I help my daughter with her homework. Making my husband's plate does not make me less powerful. No, it only serves to reveal my real power.

LOVE LIFTS

Some looking into our marriage might assume that I 'wear the pants.' I even had a friend of mine tell me her husband said he didn't want to be like my husband; he referred to him as henpecked. But what others don't see is my husband exhibiting what Ephesians 5 instructs him to do, LOVE. With love everything and anything is possible. Like the hymn goes, "Love lifted me! Love lifted me! When nothing else could help, Love lifted me".

My husband knew that if he loved me, I would one day understand that he was not there to rule me, be my daddy or tell me what to do. He knew that it was going to take his love to break down my reservations on marriage and roles. His love requires him to sacrifice his human tendency to want to be King Kong.

When Ephesians 5 told me to submit, it gave husbands a whole laundry list of action items in marriage. I only got two. My husband knew his role was just to love me. He loves our marriage so much that at times he would give up opportunities for personal gain so that I could go after my passions.

POWER AND POSITION

As I reflect on almost two decades of marriage, I understand my power can co-exist with my position or status as a wife. I was created to be half of a strong partnership divinely designed by the Creator. My husband and I are one. We are a unit. Our oneness outweighs every weakness. Furthermore, we know it is not so much who God brings together but what God brings together that no one should separate. What God brought together were my husband's strengths to complement my weaknesses and my strengths to complement my husband's weaknesses. Since we learned to approach life's challenges and opportunities as a unit, our oneness outweighs every weakness.

Problems go from bad to worse in a marriage when either or both spouses look for blame instead of blessings. When God came looking for Adam after he ate of the forbidden fruit, Adam looked to blame. Eve did the same. When it was all said and done, God forced them to find the blessing in the mess they had made. They were a husband-and-wife congregation of two when they heard God tell the serpent Eve's seed would bruise his head.

In the next chapter of their marriage, *"Adam made love to his wife Eve, and she became pregnant and gave birth to Cain. She said, 'With the help of the Lord I have brought forth a man'"* (Genesis 4:1 NIV). After Cain murdered their second son Abel, it would have been easy for them to keep looking for blame instead of looking for blessings. Fortunately, this chapter of their marriage ended in such a way that Adam made love to his wife again, and she gave birth to a son and named him Seth, saying, *"God has granted me another child in place of Abel, since Cain killed him." Seth also had a son, and he named him Enosh. At that time people began to call on the name of the Lord. (Genesis 4:25-26 NIV)* Not only did people begin to call on the name of the Lord in this chapter of Adam and Eve's marriage, Luke 4:38 tells us Seth, the third son of Adam and Eve was in the genealogy of Jesus, the offspring who would bruise the serpent's head.

The beauty of Adam and Eve's marriage is while blame marked its early days, blessings marked its latter days. When the husband and the wife recognize their strengths are intended to compensate for each other's weaknesses, they will spend less time criticizing each other's weaknesses. On my first date with my husband, I shared how Eve was made from Adam's rib. She was made out of the bone God had given him to support his upper body and protect his heart. To this day, I understand the power and position I have to support my husband and protect his heart.

Cheryl Dixon is passionate about the development of strong families and legacies.

She is a native Detroiter, and earned a Bachelor's Degree in Finance at Wayne State University, with many other real estate and finance certifications. Cheryl loves learning and believes that capturing all types of knowledge and wisdom is what balances us and guides our life.

She imparts wisdom and practical knowledge into younger women to become God's virtuous women, while encouraging all to pursue and achieve their goals with success.

She is a prayer warrior at Word of Faith Christian Center.

Cheryl is a real estate broker and a mortgage and finance practitioner, with over 30 years of experience, and is always willing to help people. She is an entrepreneur, and also likes following the stock market.

Cheryl enjoys cooking and partaking in healthy gourmet meals with her family and friends, taking long walks, boating, traveling and praising The Lord at all times.

She is a mother of 4, a grandmother of 2, and a wife of over 30 years. She has written this story with the intentions of helping others conquer serious challenges, and to know that God's word is most definitely a tool and a weapon to fight and win our battles.

Victory is ours through Christ Jesus!

The Journey of Our Life

We so often live for tomorrow, and next week, and next year, more than we live for today. We've all heard it before, that life is not any particular destination at all, but instead, a long journey. But after that day, it's now even more crystal clear that tomorrow is not always promised to us, and that each day we awaken really is "the present."

"This is the day which the Lord hath made; we will rejoice and be glad in it." (Psalms 118:24, KJV)

I've quickly learned that we must embrace everyday by grabbing hold to God's word first and love one another and have fun as we go forth, and do His will for our lives. It was August of 2016 when my husband began to complain about a hard spot in his left armpit; we thought that it would go away after a few days. However, when September rolled around he said again that this hard spot was beginning to aggravate him, even more. Since we've both always been very healthy, I didn't think much of it. We were just starting to have lots of fun right now. Our daughter had recently gained employment with the airlines, which provided us with free flight benefits. It was great.

"Every good gift and every perfect gift is from above, and cometh

down from the Father of lights, with whom is no variableness, neither shadow of turning." (James 1:17, KJV)

I don't know if the pressure from long flights causes increased problems with growths, but Jerry took a 16-hour flight to Dubai. When he returned home, the growth had increased largely in size. We didn't realize that a storm was brewing on this journey which we were about to face. This destination was not one of our choice. It started out at the hospital emergency room. We were back and forth there for three months, before the doctors would make any sense about where we were heading. We could all only agree that it was hard, large and becoming more painful every day.

However, that last doctor which we saw in the emergency room had a bright idea after looking at the growth. He was a surgeon; therefore, he determined that, whatever it was, let's just cut it off, and move forward. Unbeknown to us, cutting out such a growth or tumor without sufficient knowledge and understanding, can be very risky, dangerous, and even life-threatening.

The intense pain that Jerry was experiencing took over our thought pattern, and we went along with the surgeon, who went ahead and scheduled an immediate surgery for the following morning. That evening before, we prayed on the phone all night long, and then again, the next morning before the surgery. Before this occasion, praying for more than 30 minutes was somewhat unusual for me. As a prayer warrior, I thought that I knew how to pray. I had been trained to pray for people, but for only about 10 minutes, maximum. We learned to keep it short, to the point and effective. However, in this situation I was prompted by the Holy Spirit to just take my time, and not look at the clock and just pray, earnestly.

"Pray without ceasing." (1 Thessalonians 5:17, KJV)

The Lord was showing me that a larger arsenal of weapons and tools would be needed on this journey. We didn't realize that we were on our way into a battle. The purpose and need for the scripture in 1 Thessalonians was being revealed to me. This was not a battle that we could fight alone. On this trip, I'd also learn the importance of being equipped with swords, shields, and the whole armor of God to fight against powers and principalities in high places.

"12 For we wrestle not against flesh and blood, but against principalities, against powers, against the rulers of the darkness of this world, against spiritual wickedness in high places.13Wherefore take unto you the whole armor of God that ye may be able to withstand in the evil day, and having done all, to stand." (Ephesians 6:12-13, KJV)

We were on our way to such places, this time. By the time I arrived back to the hospital, the word of God was in action, and God had said something different. At 6:00am that morning, when the surgeon arrived, I believe that our angels entered into that room along with him. Jerry was stretched out on the hospital gurney, in only a hospital gown and ready to be taken into surgery. This was all happening much too fast. The surgeon looked at us with anticipation, to stay on schedule for day. He was serious, with only a few gestures to remind us of the possible outcomes. We were both tensed, and only sought some sort of relief.

All of a sudden, as Jerry was about to be transported to the operating room, it came out of nowhere, from the surgeon. He just blurted out, "You know what, for some reason, I just can't go through with this surgery. Go and see your main doctor." That's when Jerry and I looked at one another with dismay. The response appeared so very random. But at the same time, we were both relieved. It was as though a weight of stress was removed from our shoulders. It was the burden removing and yoke destroying power of God that interceded for us once again. I handed him his clothes and we got up and walked out of the hospital, and just smiled from ear to ear at each other. This was one of the strangest days of our lives. We were both spiritually aware enough to know that God said, not so.

"10For it is written, He shall give his angels charge over thee, to keep thee: 11and in their hands they shall bear thee up, lest at any time thou dash thy foot against a stone." (Luke 4:10-11, KJV)

We were also both convinced that the surgeon was convicted by the power of God. For he had not even obtained a single x-ray and didn't have a clue what he was about to just "cut out" of my husband. If this surgical procedure would have occurred, it would have caused a huge and life-threatening problem. However, this hard spot, which we called "the beast" was still on the prowl, and continuing to grow and cause havoc. Jerry was suffering and was now beginning to lose weight.

During our professional careers with employers, we had the best of insurance policies. While self-employed, and very healthy, we've never invested heavily in any premium health insurance policies, and only had the bare necessities for medical coverage. The basic policy fit well into the budget, especially considering we were not expecting to use it. But with such a basic and subpar policy, many doctors and hospitals wouldn't accept our insurance.

We searched high and low for a good doctor; we really didn't even have one of our own. We were so lost and didn't even know where to turn. We needed a navigation system. I'm simple enough to know that I need the Lord at every turning point in my life, and I didn't have any problem in calling on Him, once again, "Lord show me where to go and what to do."

"Thy word is a lamp unto my feet, and a light unto my path." (Psalm 119:105, KJV)

We ended up at the U of M Hospital where extensive testing and research began. We waited for answers and continued to pray without ceasing, and they provided answers quickly. They immediately advised of a stage three sarcoma cancerous tumor. Wow... I still remember that day; it was like a gut wrenching punch in the stomach. The devil quickly reminded us now of Jerry's brother, who had just passed away after a bout with cancer just two years ago. His father also had experienced lung cancer. The devil thought he had us now. Another Dixon man was in the balance, and as strong as we both thought that we were in the Lord, there was an initial shock factor there. It took us for a loop for a moment. We had to quickly shake it off. With such odds against us, there was only one thing to do...we both literally cried out to the Lord.

"And when we cried unto the Lord, he heard our voice, and sent an angel, and hath brought us forth out of Egypt: and, behold, we are in Kadesh, a city in the uttermost of thy border." (Numbers 20:16, KJV)

The pain was taking over and Jerry was not going in to work much now. I was doing double duty to keep things intact, both at home and at work. But, before we knew it, we both had not worked in months, but somehow, all of the bills and all of our needs were super naturally met.

"But my God shall supply all your need according to his riches in glory by Christ Jesus." (Philippians 4:19, KJV)

By now almost everyone, and I really do mean everyone, that was intimately involved in our lives came over to our home, bringing bags of grocery, cooked meals, catered meals, and even checks in the mail. This went on for over a year. We were shown love above measure. During this time, the Lord also provided the largest real estate closing of the year. We still, even today, don't understand how that deal actually closed. Jerry's attitude toward God's word and his healing remained positive. Since we prayed without ceasing, it kept us from wavering.

"6 But let him ask in faith, nothing wavering. For he that wavereth is like a wave of the sea driven with the wind and tossed. 7 For let not that man think that he shall receive any thing of the Lord. 8 A double minded man is unstable in all his ways. (James 1:6-8, KJV)

The hardest part throughout this whole ordeal though, was in telling Jerry's mother of his condition. Even though her intuition told her something strange was happening, we still had to break the news to her lightly. We were all very concerned because she was still grieving the loss of her other son, who was only two years older than Jerry. At home, our youngsters were wondering exactly how to proceed. I felt that all eyes were on me. I've always watched how I behave and interact with Jerry in front of them. It's important to me for them to see harmony at home. My daily goal is to set an example.

I work hard to obtain knowledge and information in the natural, but real wisdom only comes after seeking the throne of God. After crying out to The Lord, He told us that He was going to heal Jerry. In my role as partner, I was prompted to align myself with God's word and to join my faith with his. I rode on the eagle's wings with him throughout months of chemotherapy and radiation treatments. It was very daunting. But I loved and served him daily.

He had many challenging days. These treatments began to breakdown the tumor. This demon was literally now coming out of his body. It was now draining and reeking a very foul odor. I quickly became a full-blown nurse, changing bandages at least three times per day. So, we couldn't proceed too far away from home, until the surgery happened, after 6 months of treatment.

Both husbands and wives, should always treat one another right. You never know when a day may come where you might become fully dependent upon one another. Jerry has always been a kind husband, and it was actually a pleasure to serve him. I also wanted him to know, especially during this challenging period, that he was still loved by his wife. But this was not a pretty time for us. Pictures of this tumor could lead to you being sick on your stomach.

"8 Finally, be ye all of one mind, having compassion one of another, love as brethren, be pitiful, be courteous: 9 Not rendering evil for evil, or railing for railing: but contrariwise blessing; knowing that ye are thereunto called, that ye should inherit a blessing." (1 Peter 3:8-9, KJV)

> *We didn't see any light in the natural; however, in the spirit God spoke clearly to us.*

We were in a long tunnel during this journey. We didn't see any light in the natural; however, in the spirit God spoke clearly to us. I could not believe the peace that He kept us in. It was definitely beyond our understanding. He also said that He would provide rest for us. Our cousin had an empty condo right near the University of Michigan campus and offered it to us for lodging. Without that blessing we would've been left to drive 50 miles each way to the hospital on the snow filled and icy Michigan roads, oftentimes on a daily basis.

The more the doctors explained their scientific analyses and rationale on this case, the more radical we became with the word of God. One of the physicians said that this tumor reminded her of Job's condition. She was focused only on what she saw. This tumor was as severe as the boils that Job had on his body. I quickly reminded her though, that even though it looked bad in the natural, that his wife would not to tell him to curse God during this fight.

"Then said his wife unto him, Dost thou still retain thine integrity? Curse God, and die." (Job 2:9, KJV)

While continuing to focus on the word of God both day and night, and pray without ceasing, was when our faith had grown to another level, from one level of glory to another level of glory. We began to build a spiritual muscle which was able to break through the natural realm of logic. We entered into a different place, where we didn't even know how He was going to do it, but we just knew that He said it, and we believed it. Therefore, we were awaiting the receipt of our healing!

Travis Green's record, which says this very thing, was huge in convincing us of that "as our backs were against the wall, that He would deliver us, we didn't need to know how He was going to do it; we just knew that He Would Make a Way." Our wonderful bishop also laid hands on my husband and declared and decreed, and rebuked this demon of sickness out of Jerry's body. We all joined our faith together, we were putting that demon of a sarcoma cancerous tumor to flight.

"How should one chase a thousand, and two put ten thousand to flight, except their Rock had sold them, and the Lord had shut them up?" (Deuteronomy 32:30, KJV)

God also said that it was OK, to remind Him of his word, or to call Him out on the carpet, boldly and in front of others, loudly, and courageously, to a point where we sound crazy in doing so. That's when I knew that I was in "the zone," out there on a spiritual high with

Jesus, calling things out into existence, yeahhhhh. We've been on a lot of trips, but this was actually The Journey of Our Life!

"As it is written, I have made thee a father of many nations, before him whom he believed, even God, who quickeneth the dead, and calleth those things which be not as though they were." (Romans 4:17, KJV)

All of these scriptures noted above were weapons used to fight this battle in the spirit, to attain our victory. It's like my Glock in my pocket to shoot the devil with. God is real and His word gave us authority over that tumor. His word says that it had to flee, and it did.

"11 Put on the whole armour of God, that ye may be able to stand against the wiles of the devil.12 For we wrestle not against flesh and blood, but against principalities, against powers, against the rulers of the darkness of this world, against spiritual wickedness in high places.13 Wherefore take unto you the whole armour of God, that ye may be able to withstand in the evil day, and having done all, to stand.14 Stand therefore, having your loins girt about with truth, and having on the breastplate of righteousness; 15 And your feet shod with the preparation of the gospel of peace;16 Above all, taking the shield of faith, wherewith ye shall be able to quench all the fiery darts of the wicked.17 And take the helmet of salvation, and the sword of the Spirit, which is the word of God:18 Praying always with all prayer and supplication in the Spirit, and watching thereunto with all perseverance and supplication for all saints; 19 And for me, that utterance may be given unto me, that I may open my mouth boldly, to make known the mystery of the gospel, 20 For which I am an ambassador in bonds: that therein I may speak boldly, as I ought to speak." (Ephesians 6:11-20, KJV)

After this spiritual journey and warfare, Jerry is now totally healed by the power of God's word. We continue to confess His word daily. We are the healed and not the sick, and we can do all things through Christ who strengthens us. It is His will that we are healed, happy and resting in His perfect peace; celebrating! We will be celebrating our 30th anniversary and Jerry's 60th birthday this May. We are planning to take a special trip, one where we decide the destination.

After this past journey, we will be so much more grateful to travel both home and abroad. We are now reminded how blessed we've been all along.

Our words shape our lives, our future and our destinations, for sure.

Renee Flowers has a strong heart for encouraging and empowering other women and young girls. After retiring from the corporate world of P&C Insurance in August 2017, she embarked on her new life's mission to serve others as an ordained minister and a life coach.

Married to the handsome/hot Jason Flowers for seven years, they share a blended family of four children and one grandson.

Renee loves spending time with family and friends, traveling, shopping and laughing.

A native of Indianapolis, she graduated from Ben Davis High School and from Medtech College with a certificate in ICD-9 and CPT Medical Coding and Billing.

She successfully completed the 5D Coach Program with Authentic Identity Institute in December 2017 and is a first-time author. Renee is launching ILYS(Intentionally Loving Your Spouse) in the Fall of 2018 where you will have an opportunity to be Encouraged, Empowered and Inspired.

*I*ntentional Love

Communication is the key to any relationship. You've probably heard that advice countless times, but how do you do that? Some of us aren't good at verbalizing our thoughts and feelings. That was so true for me, I would be afraid to speak up, afraid that things may blow up or be misunderstood so I would just internalize my feelings. We can only go so long before things just boil over and all those things I was afraid of would happen anyway. It was on and poppin'. But praise God for deliverance. I am no longer fearful. *"For God has not given us the spirit of fear, but of power and of love and of a sound mind." (2 Timothy 1:7 KJV)*

Now, before you think just claiming one bible verse solved all that, please read on.

I met my AMAZING husband 14 years ago at a backyard barbeque on a hot summer day in July. I was reluctant to go as I was not in a good space in my life, since my first marriage was over.

My best friend kept pleading with me to come. I decided to get dressed and go. I was there, but not...I grabbed me a chair and sat kind of off to myself watching everyone having a good time as I was thinking, why am I here?

Then this fine brother came and pulled up a chair by me and started some small talk. He was funny and made me laugh, which is something I had not really done in a while considering the things I was going through. Besides my broken marriage, I had been diagnosed with depression and was prescribed anti-depressants to take. But God... I was not as strong in my faith as I am now, but even then, I knew that was not going to be my life!

I had two people depending on me; my daughter, 13, and my son, 2 years old. This fine brother just happened to be my best friend's uncle. Before you all say anything, she did not hook us up. Looking back, it was all the Lord's doing! We saw each other a few more times before we exchanged numbers. We would talk for hours. I told him I was married and separated, and filing for divorce, and I would understand if he didn't want to talk to me anymore. It didn't deter him, and a few weeks later he asked if he could take me out to lunch and a movie. Y'all already know, I accepted. And let me tell you, it was a blast! We laughed and talked and just enjoyed each other's company. It was refreshing for me. It seemed as though we had known each other for years. Once my divorce was final, things progressed, and we got married. And we still have that same kind of fun 14 years later.

Despite our easy relationship, I still had trouble verbalizing my thoughts and feelings. If this is what is happening in your marriage, you need to do two things: be patient with one another and be in prayer always.

I know you all have that burning question as to was there sex before marriage? My answer, absolutely there was. My husband and I also lived together for a few years prior to us getting married. Now, this is a no judgement zone, put them stones up...

"Let any one of you who is without sin be the first to throw a stone at her" (John 8:7 NIV).

"For all have sinned and come short of the glory of God." (Romans 3:23 KJV)

I'm not justifying sex before marriage at all nor am I condoning it. I knew it was wrong and would often cry/pray to God for forgiveness for doing it until I just got tired of repenting for the same thing. I can't point out a specific time as to when I decided I did not want to keep living that way, I just knew I wanted to do better and be better in every aspect of my life. I started reading my bible more and praying to God in that specific area and as time went on I was getting closer to God and developing an increased desire to be obedient not only in this area, but all areas of my life.

"Obedience is better than sacrifice, according to the word of God." (1 Samuel 15:22)

The Lord has forgiven me for having sex at any time in my life before marriage, for having a child out of wedlock. He has forgiven me for all of my short comings. And the Lord will and has forgiven you too. If you are currently in this state, whether you are living with someone or being physically intimate, seek God for guidance on whether this is the person he has set aside for you to be your spouse or not. If so or if not, you guys must come together and make it right in the sight of the Lord and according to his word. Know that you are worth the wait. That is what the word of God instructs us to do.

No, you don't have to "try it out first" to see what they're" working with" or to see if you're going to "like it". God knows what and who you need, what you like, and what you don't like better than you do. The Lord is equipping the right person for you and you for them. Be patient and wait on the Lord for the appointed time. The Lord is always working on our behalf and he has already hand-picked the right one for you. Trust him even in this. He will give you strength and patience.

My now husband and I talked about it and we were on the same page in knowing this was not God's way. We wanted to be married, so we did it, (even though at the time I met him, he was sure he'd never get married again). This is a second marriage for both of us. And let me tell you, it is much better the second time around!

About a year into our marriage, I fell back into a rut of complacency and fear. I wasn't being a good communicator. My husband, who is in a management position, brought home an exercise he used with employees and asked if we could try it. It was called, Start, Stop, Continue. We would write down what we wanted the other to Start doing, Stop doing, and Continue doing, then we would come together and share what we had written and talk about it. Now, let me tell you that the first several times we did this it was still hard for me! You have to be open and receptive to what the other has written as it is their honest feelings and thoughts. We would do this every couple months, and our communication got better over time.

I feel that exercise really helped us and especially me in verbalizing. And I feel it helps to bring awareness and help hold the other accountable and be mindful. We can't be better or do better if we don't know what we may be doing or saying, or even how we are saying it is affecting our spouse. Fourteen years later, we still do Start, Stop, Continue; we don't always write it down, but we do "check-in" with each other all the time and ask "How's it going from your seat? Is there anything I'm missing? Do you need anything from me?" Or something along those lines. I am no longer fearful, and I don't let things fester anymore.

For God has not given us the spirit of fear, but of power and of love and of a sound mind (2 Timothy 1:7 KJV). It's awesome and I bless the name of Jesus!

Now, we'll move on to the role intimacy and sex plays in a marriage. It is also a way to communicate reserved only for your partner. First it is important to understand the difference between intimacy and sex:

Intimacy: closeness, friendship, togetherness, rapport, warm attachment, private, cozy atmosphere

Sex: intercourse, lovemaking, the act of sexual relations

Know the difference and excel in both!

I like being intimate with my husband. One way we stay intimately connected is through prayer. We both pray for each other individually. I pray that I am the type of wife I've been called to be. God knows what my husband needs, he knows us better than we know ourselves. I ask God to reveal that to me and to help me operate in that way. Since I struggle with verbalizing my thoughts and feelings, I continue to pray that he shows me ways to love and support my husband, how to speak to him, with the right tone and the right words to say. I'm always in prayer for that. It's important that we don't fall into complacency in any aspect of our marriage.

Complacency can cause the channels of communication to suffer, causing frustration between you and your spouse. Complacency leads to emotional detachment and or potential loss of interest and possibly lead someone to venture outside the relationship. That's why the power of prayer is such an important tool to stay connected with your spouse.

In addition to our individual prayers for our marriage, we also pray together. Praying together for our marriage is an incredibly intimate act. We are agreeing to love, honor, and support one another.

Being intimate can be fun too. Sometimes I may send my husband a card in the mail or put it in his office, or I write him a note just to let him know I'm thinking about him and I appreciate him. I've put a single rose in his car, or in the fridge, or just somewhere I knew he was going to go. I may send him an invitation for date night. You can do this via text, email, mail, evite or whatever. It does not have to be anything extravagant.

> *Complacency can cause the channels of communication to suffer, causing frustration between you and your spouse.*

You don't need to buy any expensive gifts to express your love and appreciation for one another. Go out and buy some silk rose pedals (you can reuse these) and have your spouse come home to them spread out on the floor and leading from the door to the kitchen where the table is set if you've cooked a nice meal. Or you can set up a picnic area, with some blankets and pillows, candles, music. And just hang out and enjoy each other. Don't get all stressed out if funds are tight or let that deter you from "dating" or being "intimate" with your spouse. Often, it's the simple things that matter most.

And last, but not least and this may be the most important, please make a conscious effort to celebrate one another with words of admiration. We should esteem, encourage, support, and express our unconditional love for one another. And ALWAYS PRAY for one another.

Now, some of you may feel like you're stuck or in a rut in regards to intimacy/sex with your spouse. Complacency and emotional detachment, or indifference is creating that distance between you. Or you are just going through the motions.

We are not supposed to be holding out from our spouses unless there is an agreement to do so. According to the word of God in 1 Corinthians 7:1-5 (PLEASE read this entire scripture reference) with emphasis on vs. 5 *"Do not deprive each other of sexual relations unless, you both agree to reframe from sexual intimacy for a limited time so you can give yourselves more completely to prayer. Afterward, you should come together again so that Satan won't be able to tempt you because of your lack of self-control." (NLT)*

So, no more "holding out." You know I've never told my husband no. He always has access to the "cookie jar." I'm always willing and ready. This is one of the precious gifts of marriage, (remember withhold those stones, this is a No Judgement zone).

A rut could be due to a plethora of things. Our bodies change and we feel unattractive, or too tired because you're so busy with "life", or just bored of the status quo, you know, the Mary and Joseph way. (wink) At least, that's what I call it. Just to name a few.

So, I would like to share some things with you all that may help the spark/fire to come alive again. First and foremost, we have to be in prayer about ALL things. Nothing or no subject is off limits with God. He created us to be physically connected as well as emotionally and spiritually.

Now, we have to also be mindful of our spouse's sexual needs and capabilities. So you have to keep the line of communication open with one another and seek God for guidance, yes, even in your sex life with your spouse. It's ok to be creative and adventurous. You and your spouse may need to go to the "toy" store and get some toys. We did. We talked to the people there, told them we didn't want anything really crazy, but we wanted to spice things up a bit. (Communicate with each other about your comfort level.)

You may need to venture outside of the bedroom into some different places. Sometimes the "old conventional way" is boring and you need to add some spice. Do some different things like trying some new positions, fore-play, dress up, put your heels on and your sexy attire and just walk around the house like that and I guarantee there will be some fireworks!

No, no, no.... put them stones up, you are still in the No Judgement zone!

As I said before, we can seek God for an answer in every area of our lives. God said to be specific in our prayers. You know, I always pray to God that the attraction, the fire between me and my husband will never die or "cool off".

Don't you know, I still have a crush on my husband and he still gives me butterflies. Which is awesome to me. No, it's not just a physical attraction either, I am attracted to his love for God, his family and the way he serves others and the way he treats me. I am attracted to his intellect; the brother is really smart and educated. He's caring and charismatic. I am attracted to his integrity, his smile, his laugh. Of course, I can go on and on as there are so many things that attract me to my husband. He's an overall AMAZING man! I often call him my earthly "superman" or my "hero".

If you feel you've fallen into that rut of complacency, then you need to get busy. **Start** praying, **Stop** being complacent and detached, and **Continue** to look to God as your source of strength.

Use your time in prayer to seek guidance in relating to your husband, to release that spirit of fear and to be of sound mind. Be on guard against the subtle creep of complacency, instead, speak words of admiration, surprise him with a date night, a favorite meal or just a text message letting him know how much you appreciate him. And continue – one text message or one date night won't do it. It is a continual process and as you seek God, he will continue to give you both the desire and the strength to grow in intimacy, together and with him.

I will continue to seek him in all aspects of my life – don't want to fail God, my husband or myself.

Lena L. Middleton freely gives herself away to the calling of the Most High God. She is humbled by the opportunity she has been graced to behold.

Lena is the wife of Eric Middleton and mother of two college students, Erica and Lawrence Middleton.

Lena earned her B.S. in Organizational Leadership and her M.A. in Applied Sociology. With a passion for higher education, Lena spent several years as a leader in collegiate Student Affairs as well as teaching as an adjunct faculty member for local colleges. She also spent several years matriculating through the Higher Education Administration Doctoral program before accepting God's call to leave the formal education setting and serve in healthcare. As a result of that calling Lena joined the ranks of senior leadership for a healthcare organization whose focus is caring for the senior citizens of Indianapolis. Lena not only leads, but also was charged with launching two of the clinical sites in the Indianapolis region.

Lena is a licensed and ordained minister who was called to plant and co-pastor New Spiritual Life Christian Church where she is committed to preaching, teaching and following the Great Commission. With a community focus, Lena has fostered partnerships with other local pastors in events such as the Christian Debutante Cotillion, Youth Bible Institute, Peace Walks, 12 for 2 Preaching Explosion and more.

*T*here I Sat

I remember the day so vividly; there I sat, at the kitchen table. It was our first home. After a miscarriage and getting pregnant again shortly after with our daughter, my husband worked feverishly. He said, "No more renting. I'm buying us a house," and that is exactly what he did. He wanted us to have a home.

There I sat. I remember the smoky glass top on our kitchen table. I sat there looking at my own reflection. I barely recognized the person staring back at me. She looked like me, but her eyes were different. The zeal for life was gone. The zest and energy she once had vanished with three pregnancies and two babies all within the same two years. Something happened to her. She looked so sad. She looked lost.

There I sat. I was 25 years old with a one and two year old pulling on either leg. I sat there at that kitchen table wondering and building. I know hours had to have passed by, but I still just sat there. I was wondering why as I simultaneously built a horrid story in my mind. I was wondering why he wouldn't just leave, and building the scenarios of the affair that I was convinced he was having.

My insecurities and disgust with myself were at a dangerous high. My husband was an innocent target in my commitment to justify the hurt that I truly had no reason to feel. I couldn't explain it, so I just kept building it. As I was in the midst of building the end of the story, he walks in, the man who I love, the man who I said yes to, but was determined to push away. I couldn't help myself. I felt like Sybil with split personalities. One part of me knew I was tripping, but the other part of me was working hard to destroy any semblance of happiness.

I was enraged and couldn't explain why. Yes, he told me I was beautiful. He told me he would never leave. He told me I was his. But there was a story, the story I was building. The story was so real that my heart was literally breaking as I intricately placed each layer together. I was building this story with complexity. My facts were exaggerated and made up. I somehow turned one late night into hours of free time he never actually had. I was in so deep that I found the point of no return. Apart of me knew I was building the story, but the stronger voice in my head led me to believe it with everything I had. I convinced myself that I was hurt. I was not hurt by the story I built, I successfully convinced myself that my husband was the culprit behind it.

"and do not give the devil a foothold." Ephesians 4:27 "Trust in the Lord with all your heart and lean not on your own understanding; in all your ways submit to him, and he will make your paths straight"

I know Lord. You said not to give the devil a foothold. I can honestly say that I did not give the enemy a foothold. A foothold is like giving a space where a foot can be securely placed when climbing. I gave the devil an entire ledge that he could firmly plant both his slimy feet and hands.

Mentally, I went all in. I had a story to build. It was his ex-girlfriend. Yes, that was it! No, maybe it was the neighbor. She always had too many words for him each time they were outside at the same time. I made a mental note to keep my eye on her. I checked his pant pockets as I did laundry. I searched his car whenever I drove it. I smelled his shirts and examined his collars.

"Don't worry," I thought. I'll find out. I'll confirm the story building in my mind. I even went as far as to inform him that I knew he was up to something. I tried to outsmart and use creative questioning in hopes that he would stumble over his words or that I would catch him in a lie. I would get him to admit to the story I built by any means necessary.

I had officially become "that" wife. Insecurity had become my name. I was consumed with a 365-day investigation. We didn't have cell phones back then, but my search intensified nevertheless. I had to dig deeper and look harder. I searched his wallet for numbers. I searched the caller id for unknown numbers. And yes, I did call those unidentified numbers back finding myself quite embarrassed when it was one of his guy friends or a bill collector's office. I was that wife all right.

"The Lord himself goes before you and will be with you; he will never leave you nor forsake you. Do not be afraid; do not be discouraged."
Deuteronomy 31:8 (NIV)

I hear you Lord, but I was discouraged. I embraced discouragement. I had found solace in the possibilities of dysfunction. If there were a greater issue in my marriage, I would not have to focus on the issue that was truly growing within myself.

Mentally, I stayed at that same kitchen table for a solid year. I sat there looking at the reflection staring back at me from the glass top table. As time passed, I recognized that person less and less. I was losing me slowly but surely.

I didn't want to admit it, but I was jealous of the freedom I felt my husband had. I was jealous of the successes he was able to achieve. I was on that track. It should have been me. I should have graduated college. I should have had the long work hours and successful career. I should have had mandated overtime to finish important projects. I was groomed for it. I was captain of the cheerleading squad. I was a great student. I played the violin for years, earning a college scholarship. Heck, I even played with the Indianapolis Symphony Orchestra. The list goes on: beauty pageants, clubs, organizations.

Like I said, I was groomed for this. Everyone expected it from me. Although my reasoning for returning home from college was beyond my control, in my mind, I failed.

Things had always come so easily for me. If I worked hard enough, I got it. I didn't mind a little hard work; I was a competitor. I had great parents. I had a great childhood. Most of what I wanted and all of what I needed was there, but then the unexpected happened. I failed...

There I sat, a failure in my mind and a failure state of mind. The half-truths I began speaking to myself started shaping my personality. I was a college drop out. I had two kids eleven months apart. I was a baby making machine. I was a stay at home mom that didn't want to cook and clean.

I failed. In my mind it only made sense that I added a failed marriage to the list of impending doom that I was embracing. Not only was I a failure in my mind, but also I was a prisoner that felt fat, ugly, and trapped by Irish twins, two little people that wouldn't even allow me to go to the restroom alone. Each time I tried to run to the restroom for some semblance of "me" time, 10 to 20 little fingers would pop up from under the door yelling, "Mommy, what are you doing in there? When are you coming out? Can we come in?" As cute as they were, and as much as I loved them, I was lost. Lena ceased to exist somewhere back in the failure that I so wholeheartedly embraced.

What made things worse is that I felt like I had no friends at all. Nobody could understand the abysmal failure that I had become. I tried talking about it, but friends were happy we were married. Family chalked it up to postpartum, and I couldn't actually tell my mother about the story I built.

Everyone thought we had it made. We often heard, "You are such a cute family. Your kids are so well behaved. You all make such a beautiful unit." They were right. My husband worked extremely hard to provide. We had nice things. However, I felt horrible. I did have a beautiful family, but something was off. I was off. I felt as if I were living a lie. Unfortunately, the only lie was the one I was building inside my mind.

Then one day it happened. Just as promised, my husband never left me although he had to believe I was losing my complete mind. Fortunately, right before I dove off the deep end, he made two life-saving and life changing suggestions. First, he asked if I was on board with him leaving the job that kept him away. It would mean that we would have to give it all up. The new house and the cars would go. It would mean that I needed to return to work full-time; we would have more time together as a family. Secondly, he suggested that I return to school and finish my degree. He shared that he would support me no matter how far I wanted to go.

And there it was. It was honestly that instant. Something changed. The light switched on. The story I worked so hard to build suddenly vanished. I could see the hurt in his eyes. I could see that he was exhausted. I could see that he felt disconnected from his wife and children. I could see that he believed in me more than I believed in myself. I could see that my constant nagging and pressing about affairs and other women hurt him as I refused to believe in him the way he believed in me.

In that instant, the Lord showed me that while I was building a story, my husband was stressed and stretched trying to ensure we had the best of everything. I realized he had no days off. He often worked a solid month before getting one day to rest. My husband, who has worked since he was 14 to provide for others, was exhausted.

I realized that I expected him to love me like Christ loved the church, but I refused to do the same in return. Not only had I pulled out of my marriage, but I had also pushed God out of it as well. I gave the devil a foothold, a step, a ladder and an entire staircase into the middle of the marriage God gifted me with.

I misused the gift. While I know I misused it, I also knew how to get back in alignment with God and His will. I was raised in the church. I knew the Lord. I've been serving and leading devotions since I was 10 years old. God knew that I knew better, and I was ready to accept responsibility and right my wrongs.

"Trust in the Lord with all your heart and lean not on your own understanding; in all your ways submit to him, and he will make your paths straight" Proverbs 3:5-6 (NIV)

Yes, I trust the Lord, and I would love to report that all was well after my moment of enlightenment. However, many of us know that the closer we try to walk with Jesus and like Jesus, the enemy intensifies his wicked mission to steal, kill and destroy. Finding a new church home and attempting to get myself, my family and my marriage right sent that devil on a mission to destroy us. He was out to kill my marriage and nearly did.

The closer we got to God, the closer the "he" and she" got to us. There was a "she" for him, and a "he" for me. In this season, my husband and I both flirted on the brink of infidelity. Once again, the insecurities threatened my insanity. A seasoned sister once told me, "Baby, if you go looking for something you will surely find it." Well, when all my searching actually led to finding something, I set out on a mission to emotionally destroy my husband. The devil didn't have to work because I was on the job myself. The "he" for me, and "she" for him was the easy path to destruction.

One night at 2am, I was pushed to give utterance to what was happening. Once again, in Sybil like fashion I was conflicted. One voice told me to shut up and take it to the grave while the stronger voice took over. In full confessional like a priest sitting with his parishioner, I gave voice to error.

With all the confessions made in that late night hour, I just knew our marriage was over. I didn't know what to do. With the dissolution of my marriage before me, I began to panic. I didn't know where to turn. I called a girlfriend in the middle of the night as a scream and cry began to build up in my chest. I couldn't breathe.

As I struggled for the oxygen to come and fill my lungs, my heartbeat felt wrong. For the first time, my heart was out of sync. My heart was out of alignment with my husband's. I realized I couldn't breathe without him. In that moment I realized our synchronicity was necessary for me to stabilize internally. I realized at that moment more than ever that we truly are one.

All praises be to God that just as instantly as I realized it before, my husband had his own epiphany. Hours after our confessions were made; my husband took a fierce hold of our marriage and rebuked the devil! He held me and explained that our bond was forever. He detailed how we as a family would be moving forward. As he spoke, my heart began to beat in rhythm and in alignment with his once again. I could finally pull in the oxygen necessary for me to breathe. We became one all over again in that moment, an unbreakable bond that has not since been broken.

Yes, the closer we got to the Lord, the more the enemy tried to kill our marriage. The key to taking things back was as easy as the unit, us, learning our rightful places. My husband who has always been a strong and stubborn man learned what it truly means to be the priest of his home. As a wife, I learned to let go of the insecurities. I had to allow my husband to love me and allow him to lead our family. In life we often make things much more complex than they need to be. Healing and forgiveness is a process, but when we stand in our rightful places they happen so naturally.

> *The key to taking things back was as easy as the unit, us, learning our rightful places.*

As we stood in our rightful places an organic healing process ensued. We fell in love all over again. It was different than before. This love has texture. This love has a scent. This love is deeper and more meaningful than we can fully explain or comprehend. This love is everything…

"Therefore, if anyone is in Christ, the new creation has come: The old has gone, the new is here!" 2 Corinthians 5:17 (NIV)

Thank you Lord for making all things new. The old me that sat at the kitchen table was no more. The old me had finally caught up with the me God was grooming for greater. The old me stopped resenting my husband for the imaginary things he never did, and allowed us to both forgive one another for the damage we caused. The insecurities melted away as they never truly had merit to begin with. One college degree between the two of us turned into four. Mediocre jobs turned into substantial careers. The whisperers and naysayers turned into supporters and followers.

Instead of competing with my husband, I learned to simply let him lead as it is his rightful place. In doing so, his commitment to supporting and uplifting me grew to a magnitude that I cannot fully comprehend even to this day. Through college degrees and accepting my call to ministry, my husband has been right there. He cheers me on and never allows me to give up. I am human, and I do have "flashback moments." When I do, he has a gentle way of reminding me that we don't need to go there.

I truly believe that every obstacle such as my moment at the kitchen table has been a set up for every couple we've been blessed to counsel, mentor and set an example for. I often preach about 25-year-old Lena. I'm not embarrassed; I am thankful. I'm thankful that God was in the midst of it all along, and that he sent me a life partner who would share in the building of such an amazing testimony.

When asked about the key to a successful marriage, I can honestly respond, "Ensure you are both standing in place." Yes, standing in place. Standing in our rightful places with God as the center created a friendship and love that rivals everything else. We are best friends. We are lovers. We are a team. No other "he," no other "she," no other thing can come between what we have trusted God to protect.

My seat at the kitchen table is quite different all these years later. As I sit, I look around at a home. Not a house, but a home. A home that is soon to be an empty nest in the next few months. A home that is full of peace, love, forgiveness and understanding. A home that I share with the man whose heart truly beats in sync with mine.

At 25, there I sat. I sat at a kitchen table in a broken house. But today in my happy home…

Here I sit!

Chandra D. Orr, first time author, has a heart for helping women stretch beyond physical and mental limitations. She's the Co-Creator of Galore, an executive's accountability group in Indianapolis, Indiana. She was raised in Flint, Michigan, but relocated to Atlanta, Georgia where she performed in the opening and closing ceremonies of the 1996 Olympic Games. She now resides in Indianapolis, Indiana with her husband, Darrin and three children, India, Bryce, and Elle, and two grandsons, Israel and Jeremiah.

Chandra earned a Master of Science Degree in human resources and a Bachelor of Science Business Degree. Over the past 20 years, she's learned the value of resourceful human development, leading to the creation of Live4aLivin LLC, a human resources training and development consulting firm. She focuses on career mapping, personal relevance, professional presence, conflict resolution, clear communication, skills development, merit recognition, Action accountability, program implementation, opportunity maximization and culture immersion. Live4aLivin's mission is to teach individuals how to love what they do and to live the life they choose.

Chandra is a huge community builder and supporter. She is the secretary of Oxford Neighborhood Association, special events volunteer at the East 38th Street Public Library, IBE's Classic Parade Lead Media communicator, creator of McDonald's LLC Giving For Greatness Program that provides gifts for disadvantaged children, and the PTO President of Charles A. Tindley Accelerated School. She is the recipient of the 2015 Love Award from House of God for her community impact. Chandra enjoys dancing, singing and skating in her spare time.

*L*ove Growth

Weeds Are Often Planted

At age five, I sat in my life sized white cardboard box dollhouse with pink shingles. It was barely big enough for me to fit sitting on a small chair. From my playhouse window I watched my mom lead different men into her bedroom. Each time she came out she would ask if I was okay and if I needed anything. I said no because I really just wanted the men to go away and for her to be with me. The men seemed nice... They smiled at me as they entered our apartment and left with goofy looks on their faces while waving goodbye. I didn't know what was going on, but I knew it wasn't enjoyable for my mom because I'd catch her crying between visits. I remember climbing onto her lap, rubbing her hair and telling her that it was going to be okay. She'd smile and say, "ok baby girl."

Four decades later, I still remember it like yesterday. Though I didn't understand, I knew that my mom was there with me. She protected me, fed me, clothed me, and I always had a bunch of cool toys. Our home was cozy with nice furniture. My life seemed good because I didn't recall wanting for anything.

At age 14, my life was very different. Mom was there, but she worked second shift during the week. Unfortunately, she'd disappear on the weekend after she got paid. Those early feelings of safety and protection were replaced by fear and loneliness. I had two brothers and our dad was in and out of our lives. I went from care "free" to care "full" because I suddenly had the responsibility of caring for my siblings and myself. Things were already confusing, then my brothers and I noticed that our televisions, game systems, and other valuables were mysteriously disappearing. Our house was practically empty. We couldn't understand it. Eventually things got so out of control that my parents decided to tell me that my mom had a drug problem… Whoa! That was a lot for my 14-year-old mind to process. After dropping that bomb on me, it got worse. My parents physically and verbally fought constantly. The most disturbing part was that they'd make up and claim to be in love. What! LOVE? How could people claim LOVE and be at war like enemies? In my mind, I'd say, *if that's LOVE then I don't want any part of it.*

At age 16, my mom figured I'd soon be interested in boys. She'd say things like, "Don't fall in love cause you're gonna get hurt… Men ain't no good, they only want one thing… You don't need a man to complete you, you're better off on your own!" I suppose that her motivation was to protect me from living the pain that she had experienced. Her relationship with my dad was a recurring warning that I should protect my heart from men. The seed of doubt had been planted that would eventually grow into the weed that choked the beauty of love from my life.

There was nothing sweet about my 16th birthday. The more responsibility I inherited, the more I loathed the thought of having a relationship. I associated relationships and kids with stress. Commitment wasn't real to me. I dated guys in high school, but when they got too close I'd "shut down" and break it off. I did allow myself to be in a long-term relationship in college. In my heart I thought I loved the person, but I couldn't seem to actually say the words. Eventually that relationship fell apart and life moved on.

The Pruning Process Feels Awkward

At age 21, I moved to Atlanta, GA for a chance to create a new, independent, life. I needed to get to know myself. Initially I was still attached to having people around. I grew weary of the dating scene after three years of unsuccessful relationships. Oddly enough an ex-boyfriend gave me the book, *Woman Thou Art Loosed*, by Bishop T.D. Jakes. The book challenged me to get to know who I was… my likes/dislikes. See, I never felt pretty enough, smart enough and shapely enough to find and keep a man that would love me for me. I decided it was time to take the bull by the horns and learn who Chandra really was. I attended movies alone, took myself to dinner, participated in dance classes… making the effort to invest in myself. For so long my life was about the care of my brothers, so the adult me didn't know what to do and it was awkward. Day-by-day I developed more confidence. It became easier for me to cut away negative experiences that influenced my perceptions of what was possible for my life. The more I did alone, the more I began enjoying my own company.

During that time I realized that I truly wanted to be in a relationship. It occurred to me that I'd have to modify my routine in order to attract the mate I desired. For example, I decided to start cooking homemade meals at least three times a week. I cleaned out my closet to create space for my significant other. I slept on one side of the bed… sounds a bit extreme, but I needed to connect the mental part of what I desired to the physical. This lasted for about three months. The strange part was that I didn't connect with anyone during that time. There I was making changes with no tangible results… It was disappointing. I knelt at the edge of my bed to have a serious talk with the Lord. Sobbing, I told Him I was tired of dating and that I wanted to find someone who'd love me for me. My emotions were all over the place. Part of me was sad because there was no sign of Mr. Right coming my way... The other part rejoiced in anticipation of God fulfilling my request. That was Tuesday, by Friday I met my soon to be husband… God was Listening!

A Worthy Journey

At age 24, I was a performer in the opening and closing Olympic Ceremonies in Atlanta. We'd been practicing every week since

January of 1996 and the closer we got to the ceremonies, the more practices we had. Excited as I was to participate in the once of a lifetime opportunity, I was tired. The countdown to the third week in August was on... That was the first weekend that I'd have to do whatever I wanted! Woohoo! My plan for Friday was to chill. Saturday, get hair done and chill. Sunday, go to church and you guessed it... CHILL! Great plan, right?

> *Meeting Mr. Right was the last thing on my mind, but as fate would have it, he was right there.*

A friend of mine was having a BBQ that just happened to fall on the first weekend to myself...ugh. Everyone knows the way to my heart is through my stomach, so I decided to go, get a plate and leave. I brushed my hair to the back, put on some lipstick and off I went. Upon arrival, I checked the mirror and thought, "Girl you look a mess!" I laughed and kept it moving because I didn't care... I had a plan! Meeting Mr. Right was the last thing on my mind, but as fate would have it, he was right there. I got up to fix my plate and in the process picked up a deck of cards. Next thing I know, I hear this voice asking me a question. I turned my head, saw his face and drew a blank. He was handsome, with mocha skin and a beautiful smile. My heart started beating really fast! He was saying something to me, but I couldn't make it out because I was smitten. Focus Chan, Focus! What is he saying? Oh, do I want to play cards? Oh yeah, I said laughing. We played cards and then we went dancing. His name was Darrin and he called me M.C. Chan to help remember my name. That night was probably one of the best nights of my life.

"For once in my life, I finally found what I was looking to find," Lyrics from *You* by Brian McKnight.

Unfortunately, during our time he shared that he was going back to home to Indianapolis, IN the next day. I was sad, but wanted to see him again before he left. I couldn't have him leave without seeing me at my best! I rose early the next day, got my hair done and headed to see him off. He answered the door, "M.C. Chan is that you?" I said, dude stop tripping, yes it's me. He was smitten! Instead of leaving right away, he decided to stay a few more hours. During our time together I realized just how funny, intelligent, sharp, and incredibly good-looking he was.

He went back to Indianapolis, but we talked every free moment we had. After a week he said, "I love you," and without hesitation I said it back. Can you believe it? I said it back! This was the FIRST time I'd ever said it to a male that wasn't my brother or cousin. He was caring, loving, and affectionate... He put a smile on my soul and my face. Oh Lord, what am I going to do? I can't go there. Just think if I'm falling for him now based on mental and physical attraction, what will happen to my heart once we become emotionally attached? We were exclusive after dating for a month, engaged a year later, and married six months after that. So much happened during that time, but nothing could prepare us for what we were about to experience.

Darrin was raised in a two-parent home, whereas mine was broken. Our childhoods were polar opposites. It became painfully noticeable after "I do." I replayed the old tapes of what I saw and heard from my parents. Fear crept in... *What if Darrin decides to leave me, What if I'm not good enough for him, Can I really give him what he needs,* were the thoughts in my head. I also struggled with intimacy and vulnerability... Showing public displays of love and affection were too much for me. Darrin loved holding hands, kissing, and hugging. I went along with it, but on the inside I was terribly nervous and uncomfortable. I loved this man...why was it a problem? Then it hit me... I was afraid. *What if I gave him my all like I saw my mom do, only to be left with nothing? Would he reject, hurt or abuse me? No thanks! I'll just keep my feelings to myself, but how?* My husband was affectionate... That was his nature.

A month after we got married, Darrin got a job that had him away two to three days most weeks. Dealing with that and my insecurities of intimacy was a bad combination.

We were good the first couple of months, then things took a turn. The more he was gone, the more I felt the need to protect my heart and hide my insecurities. In my mind, I imagined he was with a woman that would give him all he wanted...unlimited affection. So, when he'd come home happy to see me I would down play it. I'd continue to clean and cook, barely showing any emotion. I'd be bubbling with joy inside, excited to have him back home. I wanted to run and jump all over him, but my toxic thoughts stopped me.

Before long, Darrin grew weary of that. As the months passed, he became just as nonchalant as I was...it was clear that he was checking out. By the ninth month of our marriage, we lost the strong connection we once shared. We were living in two different worlds. I was so mad at myself because I knew a lot of it was driven by my indifference. Shortly before our one-year anniversary I saw Darrin in the shower; his head was down and he seemed broken. He got dressed and wanted to talk. My heart sank because I knew what it was about. He started by saying he loved me, but he had enough. He figured we made a mistake and that maybe we weren't meant to be together. He continued to speak, but I zoned out. My thoughts were overpowering me. All I could hear is myself saying was *tell him you're sorry. Tell him that you were afraid to let him in. Tell him how much you love him!* Instead I remained silent and he walked away to another room. That night I found myself back on my knees crying uncontrollably asking the Lord to PLEASE intervene! *LORD HELP ME BREAK OUT OF THIS SHELL!* I don't want to lose my husband! Tell me what to do and I'll do it!

"But when you love someone you just don't treat them bad" – Lyric from *Where I Wanna Be* by Donell Jones

Morning came, and even though I barely slept, my spirit felt alert. *Today is the day where I'm going to set the record straight. I'm going to tell him how I really feel,* I said to myself. Darrin was in his office. I walked over and said, "Can we talk?"

He said, "yes." I told him how sorry I was for how I'd been acting and that I didn't want us to end our relationship. I told him that I loved him and that I would be more sensitive to his needs. He was so hurt that all he wanted was out. I couldn't believe it... the nerve of him! There I was pouring my heart out and he still wanted to go? *Fine then leave,* I thought, but my Spirit said *be quiet and really listen to him.*

As I allowed him to get his offences out, it pained me, but it also allowed me to see how I could really cater to his heart. I realized that he was quietly dealing with some insecurity too. All this time I saw him as this confident man, but he was taking just as much of a chance as I was taking. *Lord, help me to swallow my pride and allow you to take over. I cannot do this on my own.*

We both agreed to work it out and it was **work**. Darrin was injured by my rejection. He would be so cold at times. There were moments when he wouldn't say a word to me or even look my way. To add insult to injury, I took everything personally and became extremely needy. I hated who I was becoming! How could we begin so in love and end up estranged? I wondered if some of this was fueled by my thoughts. I knew it took two to maintain a relationship, but it was important for me to assess myself. I was aware of specific things that fear enabled. I guarded my heart to avoid being hurt, yet I attracted exactly what I focused my energy against. I learned that faith and fear operate the same… whichever one you feed will generate results. I decided to release negative feelings attached to past disappointments so I could embrace my fresh blessing from the Lord. I was determined to follow the Holy Spirit's lead, regardless of Darrin's response, and God was so on point! I would be in the middle of cooking and my Spirit would move me to go give Darrin a kiss… *WHAT? Ok.* I'd walk over, give him a kiss, and walk away. Initially, Darrin didn't say or do anything. Almost like he was ignoring me… Bummer! *It's okay Chan, let God work on him like He's doing with you.* Another time I was in bed and Darrin was up late working, my Spirit told me to get up, go massage his shoulders, and give him a hug. Again, *WHAT? I'm tired plus I don't think he wants to be bothered, but ok.* I walked into his office, massaged his shoulders, and ended with a nice firm hug. He responded by laying his head on my chest… It was magnetic! I felt a connection that was missing for a long time. That moment aligned our Spirits and we were back on track. What a blessing! It was a tough year, but we made it to our one-year anniversary together as one!

"As we stare we both seek and hope to find real love, purified" Lyrics from *Use Your Heart* by SWV

That first year was pivotal in setting the tone for how we'd interact moving forward. Those events forced us to learn how to over-communicate. It was easy to share our strengths with one another, but we learned to share our vulnerabilities too. We covered each other in prayer to strengthen our bond. The enemy hates marriages and works tirelessly to destroy them. He attacks our minds using suggestions to distract and destroy. Your spouse is not the enemy. Help your mate to know <u>whom</u> you're fighting against, <u>where</u> the war is waged, and <u>what</u> you're fighting for. God gives COUPLES the POWER to Protect, Progress, & Prosper. BE in the word & DO as the Father instructs.

At age 45, we celebrated our 20-year anniversary February 21, 2018. We've learned that it takes more than love to hold a relationship together. It takes love + trust + respect + honor AND 100% effort x 100% effort from each of us. It's about trusting God to give us the insight we need to love each other freely, openly, and unconditionally. Love is sustained by continuous growth and that's a worthy journey.

"Baby it's you, You're the one I love, You're the one I need, You're the only one I see, Come on baby it's YOU" Lyrics from *Love On Top* by Beyonce.

Tracy T. Pruitt is a servant-leader, mental health therapist, conference speaker, relationship builder and an author.

Tracy T. Pruitt is a native of Indianapolis, Indiana. Tracy credits her academic discipline to the Indianapolis Public School System and is a proud graduate of Thomas Carr Howe High School. She holds a Bachelor of Arts degree from Indiana University, a Certification in Social Work from Clark Atlanta University, as well as a Master's Degree in Counseling from Indiana State University.

She shares her story of pain, but most importantly forgiveness, as a collaborating author of A Glimpse of God's Glory. Tracy combines her years of counseling expertise, with a passion for empowering, encouraging and educating women across the country.

Mrs. Pruitt holds numerous civic roles and responsibilities throughout Central Indiana. She has received several awards and acknowledgments for her outstanding professional and community involvement.

As a licensed minister, Mrs. Pruitt worships and serves at Living Water Fellowship Church of Indianapolis, Indiana, under the senior teachers and administrators, Pastors Steve and Kim Outlaw.

Tracy is an avid learner who enjoys fashion, traveling, and giving back to the community. In her spare time, she enjoys spending time with her friends and family.

Tracy is married to Dale R. Pruitt and is the mother of four adult children and a teenage son.

The Battle Was Not Ours but We Won the War

We had talked for what seemed like hours. The #42-Studio Fix was caked on the buttons of that white cordless phone. The buttons looked like malted milk duds. It was a chilly December night in Georgia. However, the room was warm and the phone was even hotter. We giggled like two middle school kids. We completed a confirmation checklist dating back to my previous visit to Indianapolis. We knew we would be married. My stomach started to tickle. My already warm face got even hotter.

This was it! I had fasted, prayed, named it, claimed it, put seed on it and trusted God. My husband, the man that I had prayed for year in and year out, he was the one that God had ordained for me. I sat on that green and burgundy couch rocking back and forth like Ms. Sophia, from The Color Purple. As we continued our conversation, I hung on every word. The tickle in my stomach started to become a pang. It hit me like a hurling dodgeball right in the pit of my stomach. I would have to tell him my truth. I had to share my testimony. "And they overcame him because of the blood of the Lamb and because of the word of their testimony," (Revelations 12:11 NASB) My testimony had been safe. My testimony was five hundred and fifty miles away. For the first time in our conversation, I felt uncertain. I had to share my real, seedy, raw testimony. The first battle began.

Battle of Truth

I was operating in my calling leading the young women's ministry at my church. I would often share my testimony with other young women of what God did in my life. I had even shared with him about the goodness of Jesus. We never got deep into our past, the thing that really led us to God. For the first time, I wondered if he could accept, if he could handle my truth. Ooh wee my truth was not pretty. Frankly, it was downright trifling. He could hear a change in my tone. In fact, the entire atmosphere changed. The room became quiet and chilly. The sweaty phone that held my running foundation was now ice cold. The battle of truth. Do I tell the entire truth? How do I explain to him that I was the woman that Jesus met at the well?

My mind was racing, my body was clammy and I was inadvertently picking the threads out of my rich green and burgundy couch. He cleared his throat and asked me, "Are you ok?" I said "Yes." He said, "You got quiet." I said, "I know." Speaking up, I said, "I need to tell you something." "What?" he asked. "Are you sure, we are called to be together?" I reluctantly asked. He said, "Yes, I know I want to spend the rest of my life with you." Slowly I spoke and said, "You may not want to be with me after I tell you this." Clenching the phone, I started to share my story. I told him about my promiscuity and how I used sex as a manipulating tool to get what I wanted and what I thought I deserved. I told him, truly, I was delivered. However, moving back home would force me to look my past in the face. The phone went silent. He spoke. His words were few but strong, "It is under the blood." It was true; it was under the blood. That battle was won. My past was not a secret the enemy could use to haunt me.

Family Battle

We settled into our new home in the suburbs of Indianapolis. It was a culture shock for the children, a big difference from Atlanta, Georgia. I no longer led our home. I had to learn to submit. I was still a strong woman, but my strength lied in learning to submit to the new headship, my husband. That was very hard. However, I was so happy to be Mrs. Dale Pruitt that I took this challenge head on; I wanted to be a good wife. I cooked, cleaned, helped with homework, and gave my new husband his dessert every night. This was our routine Sunday through Saturday. I served so much dessert that a cake started to bake. Yes, three weeks after getting married a cake was baking in my oven. I was pregnant. We were shocked. We had talked about having a baby but not this soon. While preparing for this new baby we were still trying to learn about each other. We were still trying to decide what side of the bed each person preferred. This was all happening so fast.

> *I was still a strong woman, but my strength lied in learning to submit to the new headship, my husband.*

We had a new normal and a baby growing in my over thirty-year-old body. I was trying to balance a career, being a new wife, mother, and pregnant woman. This battle got so intense that I ended up on bed rest mid-way into my pregnancy. It was announced that I was in pre-term labor and my pregnancy was high risk. Two weeks into my bed rest, I gave birth to a twenty-six week premature baby boy. The medical staff was very clear that it would be a miracle if he lived. We prayed and trusted God. He was released from the hospital the day before his original due date. God proved to be a healer and faithful to His word. With only ten months into our marriage, we had a baby and were still trying to make some sense of our life.

The doctors assured us that everything would be ok. They told us he had a few developmental delays but with the proper interventions, things would be fine. I was good with the prognosis. I had spent time early in my career working with children with developmental delays. I gave my husband hope based on the progress I saw with other children. During the first three years of his life, we got him all of the help he needed. He started to advance in so many areas and we were proud. We paid attention to the progress and overlooked his fixations. He fixated on the ceiling fan, on his racecars, the tags in his clothes that bothered him and the loud music that made him hold his ears. We did not notice some obvious signs. It was not until he was having trouble in kindergarten that we decided to take him in for psychological testing. The test came back stating that our child was diagnosed on the Autism Spectrum.

How did this happen? How did my family get into this battle? Why did God allow this to happen to us? We did everything right. We waited until we were married to have sex. We served in ministry. We treated each other right. I was learning to submit and he loved me as Christ loved the church. Why this battle?

Battle of Fear

I had dedicated my life to working with other people's children. I prided myself in being a good mother. I understood children. I knew how to help them socially, emotionally, and intellectually. I gave professional, spiritual, and personal advice to my friends and foes on what to do for children. Now it was our child. For the first time in our marriage, I felt a fear that I could not shake. I was so fearful that I became numb—a paralyzing numb. I was numb while operating in day-to-day life. I wanted my husband to save me from my fear. The problem is that he was unaware that I was living in fear. I wanted him to do what only God could do. That day I secretly started holding him responsible for emotional healing. I went into survival mode trying not to allow fear to immobilize me. I took our son to all of his appointments, therapy sessions, and school meetings. *"Do not fear, for I am with you; Do not anxiously look about you, for I am your God. I will strengthen you, surely I will help you, Surely I will uphold you with My righteous right hand." (Isaiah 41:10* NASB) Because I did not acknowledge my fear, I fed my fear with resentment. I ate resentment like a bowl of my favorite ice cream.

Silent Battle

Full of fear and resentment, I entered a silent battle. This by far was the scariest battle because it was not communicated. I allowed the enemy to feed me the same fruit that Eve ate in the garden. I ate the fruit of deception. The enemy started speaking to me, telling me that I am used to a man not taking care of my emotional needs. He told me that my husband was too focused on other things. I wore this silent battle like a child carrying a new backpack. This battle became a part of me. I carried this battle to work, to our children's basketball games, in our bedroom, in our scripture reading, prayer life and yes, even to church. It was silently sucker-punching me and no one knew it. Everyone was functioning while I barely existed.

My children were doing well in school and my husband was working hard. As instructed in the Word, he led us in prayer and served unselfishly in our church. However, he made me sick; I could not stand the sight of him. Him, the man God gave to me, the man I believed God for, was on my nerves—the last one. That little irritating voice started talking again, "He is praying for you and don't even know what you need." Continuing to eat the bowl of resentment, I wanted him to know I was scared, mad, and felt unprotected. I let fear and resentment keep me silent.

Battle of Manipulation

"For God has not given us a spirit of timidity, but of power and love and discipline." (2 Timothy 1:7 NASB) While this scripture is true, I was living contrary to what it said. I entered the battle of manipulation. I attempted to take an old weapon into a new battle. I used the weapon of sex. I thought if I would give him what he loved, which was sex, sex and more sex, he would fill the emptiness I was feeling as a mother. The emptiness was still there. In fact, I became angrier. My needs were not being met and I was feeling used. He still never addressed my fear as a mother, my feeling of inadequacy, my resentment, and now my feelings of being used. I was fed up and I was done. I had lost my confidence. I was holding my husband hostage. He was a prisoner of a war he knew nothing about. I had made up my mind I was leaving. I wanted out of the marriage.

The Battleground

The battle was in my mind, but on Friday night after our usual date, it was hitting the ground. I had already played out in my mind how I would say it and what would be the next steps. I contacted my accountability partner. Not wanting her advice, I just wanted her to hear it from me, my version, the truth. Ok, insert a laugh right now. She and her husband loved my husband and me. They wanted to see us win. They often told us how fond they were of our love for God and each other. She had always been the voice of reason for our marriage and I truly could be honest with her. She always gave me the truth in love and met me at my point of need. She asked me how we were handling the news about our son. I confessed that it was rough.

I disclosed that I was leaving my husband. I told her I was fearful, resentful, scared, and unprotected. She asked me if I thought he stopped caring about me. I said yes. I told her I was tired of pretending and that the marriage was over. She asked me had I told him what I needed from him. I got silent. She then asked if I had ever considered that he might be fearful himself. She asked me if I ever thought that he did not sign up for this either. As she talked, I was rolling my eyes up in my head, much like Beyoncé in her music video, looking unbothered. I reluctantly listened to the sound advice she gave. She reminded me that God knew we could handle this. He would not put us in this battle for us to lose. She asked me what it would look like to my children if I chose to give up. For the first time, I thought about our children. I also thought about the single, married, and young people we had encouraged about relationships. Nevertheless, I was still leaving.

We were coming home from our Friday night date. We pulled in the driveway and I told him I wanted to talk, really talk. He said ok. I told him that I needed my husband. I told him I did not want the minister, servant, or military man. I told him that I needed to talk to my husband. He turned the car off. I said we have been talking for months but not communicating. I told him I needed to communicate with him. He turned his whole body around looking me square in my face. I told him I was unsure how this conversation was going to end, but I needed to be honest with him. His eyebrows began to raise. He cleared his throat and said ok. I told him that I wanted to leave him. I told him I was unhappy and I felt all alone. I began to cry and told him I was scared. I felt like a failure as a mother. I did not know what to do for our son and I felt that he had distanced himself from me. I told him I gave him everything he wanted and he left me out there to fend for myself. I went on to tell him that he promised me that he would take care of me and he was not keeping his promise. As I was pouring out my heart, I gazed at him and his eyes were wet. He was studying my face, allowing me to pour out my heart.

True to his fashion, he spoke few words. He said, "I am scared." I got quiet. He said that he had been scared from the day he was diagnosed. He reminded me that I had told him everything would be alright. He went on to talk about his vows to protect me. He told me he had been praying, asking God how to meet my needs, while trusting God to heal him from his own fears. He said he was sorry. He said he should have communicated to me how he was feeling.

At that moment, I realized I wanted my husband to do what only God could do. I put the responsibility on my husband to heal my hurt. I made a decision about my marriage without including my husband. My lack of vulnerability almost caused me to abort my assignment as his wife. I was scared and I let my fear cause me to view my husband through foggy lens. We embraced each other and I heard the Holy Spirit speak. The Holy Spirit said, "Please give it to me." For the first time in this war, I turned it completely over to the Lord. Instantly, things with our son got better. He started doing well in school, participating in sports, and growing to understand his diagnosis. In addition, a peace came over our entire home. We didn't realize the effect it had on our children until the change happened.

Victory Battle

My husband is in the military. He shared with me the tactics the military uses when going to war. He told me to defeat the enemy and win a war, the military shuts off the communication and the food supply of the enemy. This tactic is used so the enemy has no way to communicate with each other or their allies. We used the same tactic as the military. We silenced the voice of Satan and did not allow him to feed us the spirit of deception. We had to let God take over the situation. *"And if one can overpower him who is alone, two can resist him. A cord of three strands is not quickly torn apart,"* (Ecclesiastes 4:12 NASB)

We made a conscious decision to keep fighting. We use this same tactic when we face other battles in our marriage. When praying and coaching other couples, we give this same advice. It brings us great joy to be allies for other marriages. We have recognized that had we not been honest about our fear and reservations, we would not have made it through that battle. We would have aborted the mission. *"But thanks be to God, who always leads us in triumph in Christ, and manifests through us the sweet aroma of the knowledge of Him in every place."* (2 Corinthians 2:14 NASB)

To the reader, this is a fixed fight. You have the victory because God has never lost a war. You will have battles. Some battles will challenge your faith. Find your allies that will pray with you, intercede for you, and hold you accountable to the vows you made to God and each other. Listen and follow the instructions of the Holy Ghost. Do not give up and do not give in. *"Do not fear or be dismayed because of this great multitude, for the battle is not yours but God's."* (2 Chronicles 20:15 NASB)

Tisha Reid is passionate about helping women maximize their strengths and operate within their purpose. She is recognized as a women's health advocate, community mobilizer, and anointed preacher of the Gospel. She has impacted many lives through life changing workshops, coaching, health programming, and powerful preaching.

A native of Indianapolis, Tisha is a graduate of Cathedral High School and holds a Bachelor of Science in Public Health from Indiana University. She received her license to preach in 1999 and was ordained in 2004 in Christian Ministry. Currently, Tisha serves as Associate Pastor with Uplift Church in Indianapolis, Indiana where her husband, Rodric K. Reid is Senior Pastor. In addition, she leads their women's ministry and hosts a broadcast, "Power Points 4 Living" on periscope.tv.

To her professional credit, Tisha has developed community health programming addressing health equity for over 20 years. Currently, she is the Associate Director for the National Center of Excellence in Women's Health at Indiana University School of Medicine. She serves on numerous state-wide boards and is a member of Alpha Kappa Alpha Sorority.

Tisha is an entrepreneur, providing organizational training and certified health and wellness coaching for individuals and organizations. She holds a certification in mental health first aid and is a published author. Tisha loves spending time with her husband and their three gifted daughters, Jasmin, Tiffani and Jessica. Tisha Reid is simply a child of God, serving the community, so she can hear God say, *"Well done my good and faithful servent...well done."*

*O*pen Your Gift and Reclaim Your Voice

One day in October 1990, I received a call from my sister Michele asking me to call her friend, Rodric. "I've never heard him like this before. Please call him and talk with him," she pleaded. I told her I would call; but, I really didn't feel right calling a man I didn't know. Persistent, she called me on the hour to see if I had followed through on my promise. Eventually, I expressed the reason for my hesitation. Again, with deep concern in her voice, she said, "If anyone could reach him, you can." After a brief conversation with God, I finally called him.

He was emotionally distraught over losing his gifted 17 - year old cousin to gun violence. Our first conversation was one filled with love, peace, renewed hope, and the Word of God. That night, communication through others, God, and each other became our introduction to love that has withstood the toughest of times for over 27 years.

Communication: The Key Ingredient

Communication in marriage is the key ingredient to having a viable and successful marriage. Some would like to toss this ingredient aside like its sugar in a recipe and substitute something else. We may be able to substitute sugar in recipes; but we cannot substitute communication in marriage. Gifts, parties, ministry, sex (although it's a form of marital communication) cannot be substitutes for the sharing of our voices.

Communication is so important that in the Book of Genesis - in the "Beginning," God gave us the gift of life and then he gave us the gift of communication. God gave us the opportunity to communicate with Him and creation daily. We were created to commune and share everything with God. As it is in a marriage, we should commune, spend time with our spouse, and share with them everything.

I remember when my husband and I stayed on the phone for hours. We shared our hopes, dreams, feelings, and even our daily experiences. You might be able to relate to this scenario: "You hang up … no you hang up; I love you … I love you more." Our communication was full of us sharing and expressing our wants, fears, aspirations, likes and dislikes; it was uninhibited and enjoyable by both. We looked forward to it! It was key to bringing us together. It was so good that we thought we knew everything we needed to know about one another, and decided to spend the rest of our lives together in marriage.

The Silent Years

After we were married, somehow our voices grew silent. With the concerns of the world and limited knowledge of one another, slowly the communication candle that was once so bright began to dim. With a distorted perception of how marriage was supposed to be, I allowed the enemy to instill fear. I allowed the enemy to run communication interference through the cares of the world, the television, ministry and the responsibility of our children to diminish my voice. I feared speaking my truth to keep peace. I allowed fear and my distorted view of marriage to steal my voice;

> *I lost a piece of me that my husband fell in love with and I didn't know how to get me back.*

creating an atmosphere of silence. Something my husband never asked for. The authentic voice that brought my partner joy, peace and purpose; that voice that spoke of dreams was no longer heard. I lost a piece of me that my husband fell in love with and I didn't know how to get me back. I was too busy trying to do the duties of wife and mother, that I forgot my husband was my best friend.

The more my voice became silent, the more it became the "normal." The more my voice remained silent, the more the piece of me that was lost, I was no longer looking for. With routine silence, talking "to" moments replaced talking "with," moments throughout our daily schedules of jobs, taking care of the family, and working in ministry. I'm sure you know that this "normal" is not normal for a healthy marriage. It lacked the true essence of the key ingredient. Plus, God doesn't expect us to be normal. We were created as a peculiar people destined for greatness. He made each of us unique, with a purpose and a voice to be a blessing.

We must understand that if we allow the enemy to control our emotions and keep us busy with things that appear to be important - things society tells us are important- we forget that God put us (husband and wife) together for His glory; and our relationship suffers. We have to open daily the gift of communication God gives us with our spouse.

We can't hide it, save life changing topics for another day, toss it out or give it to others. We are to share everything with one another. Some wisdom provided by our grandmothers, Nana's and others might have told us, "What he doesn't know won't hurt him." That's a lie from the pit of hell! It can and it does hurt. Moreover, if we don't talk with our spouse as God created us to do by communing/sharing everything with them; someone else may give them their ear. Or, our closed mouths may produce zero opportunities, dreams deferred, or worse: a relationship stretched beyond the silence.

Let's not position ourselves to give our spouses over to someone else for emotional communication. Also, please don't give your voice to the enemy. Don't let him silence the gift that God has ordained for your marriage. If you have been silenced, it stops today. It's not too late. Don't let your silence be the tool that separates. Go find the God - given gift that was tossed aside or buried, and open it up. I understand that it's necessary to talk to your spouse as the provider, the business partner, the ministry leader, the house manager, the parent of your children; but, don't forget to open the gift of communication that was ordained only for your spouse, your best friend.

Know the Language

In marriage, there are a variety of ways to communicate. We communicate physically, emotionally and verbally. During my silent years, one of the best books I came across on communication was *The Five Love Languages*, by Gary Chapman. He states there are five languages: receiving gifts, quality time, words of affirmation, acts of service, and physical touch in which we demonstrate our love. In other words, we need to know what moves our spouse, how they prefer to be loved. Knowing this helps us communicate with their physical and emotional needs.

Do you know what your language is? Your spouse's language? Most times, you and your spouse do not speak the same love language. During the silent years, I did not know that my husband's love language was acts of service, while mine was physical touch. I was a hugger and I liked to be in one's space. I kept trying to love my husband the way I wanted to be loved; the way I saw my parents love or the fantasy relationship I viewed on television. It didn't work and since my voice had been diminished, I never asked him what he needed. There were times he told me, but I still tried to love him my way.

Did I say it never worked? I could cheer my husband by telling him how good he was. He would be appreciative, but it didn't really move him. We both expressed our love in languages that were not bad, just not in the languages that moved us.

We must work to understand what moves our spouse, so we can better meet their physical and emotional needs. One successful example of speaking my husband's language happened this past

January when I bought him tickets to the Lalah Hathaway concert. Lalah is one of his favorite singers. The fact that I remembered his favorite singer and surprised him was an act of service that really moved him. He texted and called me on more than one occasion excited like a child going to Disney World!

Rediscover your love language. It might even change as you grow older together. Mine started with physical touch and now has evolved to include quality time. Knowing each other's language is important for your spouse and your children. Children have their own language too. Get to know how they need to be loved, so your whole household can be healthy and filled with effective, loving communication.

Divine Language

In the Bible, 1 Peter 3:7(NKJV) says: *"Husbands, likewise, dwell with them with understanding, giving honor to the wife, as to the weaker vessel, and as being heirs together of the grace of life, that your prayers may not be hindered."*

To dwell with his wife means the husband really comes to know his wife by living together physically and emotionally. In order for him to fully know and understand her, they both need to share everything and actively listen to one another. Spending quality time with one another, sharing voices, and all the relations that marriage is ordained to encompass is how a healthy, Christian marriage mirrors the marriage with Christ.

A healthy marriage is one where communication is authentic and three-way. It includes both individuals and God. It is talking, listening, and acting. It's God's divine language for marriage that does not provoke one another with railings against railings, with yelling against yelling; but, it is one that communes with one another in love, understands with a tender heart, and is non-controlling or fault finding. There may be times when couples will have disagreements. However, it should not be the "norm." It is during these times when we have to come out of our feelings or a need to be right, and implement a divine technique that the world calls active *listening* skills.

We must listen carefully to the information being said and what is not being said to get an understanding of the real message. We should speak with love during disagreements, without need for regret. Remember, life and death are in the power of our tongues. Don't let your emotions speak for you. Examine yourself, pray, and speak life into your spouse, your children, and over every facet of your family. Strive for God's divine language within your relationship. The language where prayers are heard and answered; and, being joint heirs is actualized.

Speech Therapy

If you've ever experienced losing your voice, not speaking your spouse's language, or totally forgetting to inject God's divine language, speech therapy may be in order. When I was a child in grade school, I was very talkative; but, only my mother could understand me. She knew my language. One of my teachers said I was intelligent, but school staff couldn't understand what I was trying to communicate. She suggested I go to speech therapy. In therapy, I had to practice moving my mouth differently, intentionally producing a voice with diction that others could understand. Later, in my marriage, I had to go to speech therapy again. I had allowed the enemy to still my voice so much that it also interfered in others areas of my life, including my call to ministry. It took me nine years to answer the call, only because I lost my voice and didn't have a conversation with my husband. When my maternal grandmother died, her words about my initial sermon rang in my ear, "You did well, but you were fearful and didn't give all of you. Give all of you." Since that time, I asked God to help me regain my voice.

I needed speech therapy because I had a voice for my husband, for my children, and a voice that God wanted others to hear. I began to intentionally practice or start conversations with my husband. Sometimes, I would intentionally think about what I would talk about in a car ride or when he came home from work. I intentionally spent more time with our children and I asked for more opportunities to minister. Speech therapy was necessary. I needed to practice speaking differently if I was going to reclaim my voice.

This time, God was my therapist and my mind was the assistant. God trained me through His Word and my mind was renewed. As the Bible states, I needed to: let the mind that was in Christ Jesus be in me (Phil 2:5 NKJV). To speak those things over my marriage as though they were. I proclaimed daily bible affirmations and prayers: *"I can do all things through Christ who gives me the strength (Phil. 4:13 NKJV). "No weapon formed against me or my husband shall prosper" (Isaiah 54:17 NKJV)*; and this too shall pass." Declaring through financial hard times that God *never saw his seed begging bread (Psalm 37:25 NKJV)*. Thanking God that our desire was only for one another and what God had put together no man could put asunder; even if that man was one of us in our silence or bitterness. One of my favorite scriptures I prayed over my husband for years and enjoyed seeing its fruit is:

"For this reason we also….do not cease to pray for you (Rodric), and to ask that you (Rodric) may be filled with the knowledge of His will in all wisdom and spiritual understanding; ¹⁰that you(Rodric) may walk worthy of the Lord, fully pleasing Him, being fruitful in every good work and increasing in the knowledge of God; ¹¹strengthened with all might, according to His glorious power, for all patience and longsuffering with joy; ¹²giving thanks to the Father who has qualified us(Rodric & Tisha) to be partakers of the inheritance of the saints in the light. ¹³He has delivered us (Rodric & Tisha) from the power of darkness and conveyed us into the kingdom of the Son of His love, ¹⁴in whom we (Rodric & Tisha) have redemption through His blood, the forgiveness of sins"(Colossians 1:9-14 NKJV).

Exercising my voice, going through "speech therapy" has made my dim candle shine brighter. It let me be a witness to God's glory as God heard our voice and saw that our family never went hungry or cold when my husband was unemployed. God took us from a rat-infested home to a house that our forefathers dreamed of. We started taking annual trips together, in and out of the country, to places like New York, Cancun and Dubai. Now, I can go out to eat with my husband and know that our cell phones, the host, or a plate of food will not take over our communication time. We will not be the elderly couple in MCL restaurant eating in silence. We decided that marriage is work, ever-evolving and worth every minute of therapy time.

FACE

Communication is intimate. Think of FACE when going through your own speech therapy to reclaim your voice. Face to Face is intimate. It requires quality time without televisions, social media, video games, or work. FACE can be remembered this way.

F - Friend - Your spouse should be your best friend (if they're not already).

A- Acknowledge, Act & Ask - Acknowledge God in everything. Trust Him to be the glue, open doors and to restore your marriage - your voice. Actively love. Apply the things you've learned. Act by letting the Holy Spirit lead you. Ask questions for understanding, do not assume.

C- Commune daily. Share everything. Intentionally spend quality time. Work is not more important than marriage and your first ministry is at home.

E- Evaluate & Enjoy each other. Evaluate your communication. You may be the one who needs therapy, not your spouse. Together, evaluate your finances, your vision, your love languages on a regular basis and then enjoy one another's company. Enjoy your best friend.

Opening the Gift

Open up the gift of communication ordained for marriage. Share everything. Speak tenderheartedly, utilizing active listening skills, communicating to the physical and emotional needs by speaking your spouse's language. Once you open your gift of communication, you will realize that there is some "assembly required." This type of assembling may mean that you try some of the following.

- Have a date night, no matter how many years you've been married.

When you stay at home and watch TV that's good. However, try sitting on the couch, snuggled up, talking about your dreams. Let your voice ring as you discuss your aspirations, love, favorite movie, or where you see each other in the next five years.

- Go out to dinner and have your talking points in mind, so you're not staring at one another, eating food and checking the cell phone.
- Try placing little notes in a lunch box; on the bathroom mirror; in the car; or at work. Let your spouse know that you're thinking about them.
- Intentionally engage in foreplay. Foreplay starts early in the day...a phone call, text at work, or words of affirmation/ compliments. Every now and then reverse the role and do something special for them.
- Tell your spouse what you like in the bedroom.
- More listening and doing. God's love has always been thoughtful, about action and benefited the whole person. Duplicate God's love in your marriage.
- Intentionally speak your spouse's language once a week.
- Set up an appropriate time (monthly, quarterly, annually) to review personal and family visions, budgets, and dreams for retirement, etc.
- Set a time limit for social media or technology.
- No tablets or cell phones in bed!
- Consider seeking outside counseling if needed.
- Pray together at least once a week.

If you do not remember anything else, please remember that communication is a gift from God. It is authentic, without fear, without railings, involves active listening and speaks the language benefitting the whole person. It is ultimately intimate.

Reclaim your voice, actively love, and keep moving forward by opening the gift that God gave us daily. We did. To God be the glory!

 **Myasha L. Smith-Edmonds,** a native of Houston, Texas, is the first female African-American Next Generation McDonald's Owner/Operator and Board Member in the Indianapolis region; earning the Award of Trailblazer for the National Association of Women Business Owners (NAWBO Indianapolis) and recipient of the Galore "Distinction Award".

At 13, Smith began working at her father's McDonald's where she developed her strong work ethic, accountability, discipline and focus. Smith graduated Magna Cum Laude from University of Houston with a Bachelor of Arts in Accounting and minor in African-American Studies. Smith went on to become a Certified Public Accountant completing her internship at Deloitte & Touche; one of the largest accounting firms in the world.

During her career development years, Smith earned various awards with KCOH Radio Station and numerous more as an Independent Business Owner with Ameriplan USA. Committed to helping others build their businesses utilizing biblical principles, Smith was awarded the honor of becoming the youngest National Sales Director and earned the privilege of speaking on several panels during the yearly Ameriplan National Conventions.

In 2008, Smith embarked on her ultimate dream; following in her father's footsteps and becoming a successful McDonald's Owner. During her required 2-5 year program, which she completed with highest honors on every level, she became a General Manager and was awarded the Ray Kroc Award; given to the top 1% performers in the McDonald's system.

Smith is grateful, and is inspired to continue to be a blessing to others and the Kingdom of God. She is a public speaker and has a genuine heart and special love for children; coordinating community give-a-ways with local businesses and avidly supporting empowerment youth programs like Ladies of Great Purpose and the Positive Black Male Association "Reaching Youth Everywhere RYE Program".

Mastering Marriage

Relationships usually go through four phases. The first phase is when we're so happy and in love; thinking, "where have you been all of my life." This is considered the Happy, Perfect, Ecstasy or Honeymoon phase. The second phase is when we realize that our mate is human, with problems, issues, baggage and flaws, that were not known initially. This is considered the "It's Real," Reality phase. The third phase is the tough, "Make it or Break it" phase. This is when we both are going through the storms of the relationship. This is considered the Challenge, Test or Obstacles phase (this phase will happen, continuously in any relationship). The way we handle the storms, will determine what level four will be. If we lean on our own understanding and handle them with spiritual immaturity; then phase four will be called, The End; but if we Trust God and allow him to order our footsteps, then phase four will be called, Victory (Life Long Relationship – Growing Together)!

Many think that marriage is the same as parenting, that there's no playbook; but there is a playbook. It's called The Bible. "*The LORD directs the steps of the godly. He delights in every detail of their lives. Though they stumble, they will never fall. For the LORD holds them by the hand.*" (Psalm 37:23-24 NLT)

Do I Really Know My Man? Do I Really Know...Myself??

There are so many times that couples are blinded by the joy of new love and never open their minds to the reality that marriage will not always be joy, hugs, love, respect, and kisses. We are human; we change as people, and life happens. There will be storms, peaks, valleys, trials, and tribulation in every marriage. No marriage escapes challenge, test, and pain. All of these problems come to serve a purpose in your marriage, to take you to a higher level of blessings in your life; if you stand together, stay together, overcome the devil, and allow God to have his way in your marriage. One way to HELP with this battle and to help not turn to alcohol, divorce, drugs or extramarital affairs to deal with a troubled marriage, is to have counseling. I highly recommend getting premarital counseling before getting married. If you're already married, seek spiritual counseling.
In counseling, you both have the opportunity to think, express your thoughts and open your mind to the various aspects of marriage. So, many times, we as women tend to believe that marriage is simply about us meeting the right person, the perfect person, MR. Right.... But, that's really not all that it's about. Marriage was made by God. It says in Genesis 2:18 NKJV, The Lord God said, it is not good that man shall be alone; I will make him a helper comparable to him.

We as women are the missing piece to the puzzle of their lives. In marriage, we are to follow Ephesian 5:21 NIV, *Submit to one another out of reverence for Christ.* Mutual submission is important to making a marriage work. "Building Blocks to a Strong Marriage" (Martin R. De Haan II).

> *Marriage is being a servant and having a servant spirit to one another.*

Marriage is being a servant and having a servant spirit to one another. It is understanding, it is loving to be considerate, compassionate or give in to the other's need. It's caring about each other's hurts and vulnerabilities. It's give and take, not just take. It's about prayer with and for one another. It's about the purpose and destiny that God has for both of your lives.

We should compliment, encourage, uplift, edify, inspire, help, and motivate one another to be the best that we can be in life and help ensure the fulfillment of our true potential being realized (our destiny and purpose - personally and together). In doing this, it will bring happiness, fulfillment and balance into your life and marriage.

During this process, it may bring up things that have been hidden behind the walls of pain or shame from childhood; that could explain fears, which are expressed normally in the form of anger, violence, unintended submission, lack of trust, rejection, denial, lies or silence. In these moments, it allows you both to find the person that you may have abandoned as a child, because you wanted to erase those parts of your lives. Discovering why you are, how you are, is powerful because it allows you to be in control of your life, emotions, and decisions. In revealing these mysteries in your lives, it will help you both in having a better understanding of one another. Why does he act like this or that? Why do you act like this or that? Now, instead of operating from a place of fear, hurt, abandonment, rejection, abuse or pain; you can operate from a place of power, confidence, boldness, empathy, understanding, and strength. Not allowing the past in both of your lives to determine your future. Allow it to be the pebbles of pain that you stand on to rise higher. At least, if you know you can do something about it; before it could potentially destroy your marriage. Also, in time, your mate may begin to change into someone that you have never seen before, and when this happens this is not the time to argue, fuss, and fight. This is the time to pray, communicate, listen, and gain understanding of their truth and needs.

Counseling allows you to honestly and openly discuss the realities of marriage, for example:

1) Do you view Finances in the same way?
2) The Goals, Plans, and Vision for the marriage
3) How to handle it when you learn that he can be stubborn, angry, depressed or easily hurt/offended?
4) Does he not want children, while you're intending to be a mother of five?
5) Knowing that we must show respect for our husbands in our Attitudes and our Actions

6) How to communicate and work through conflict
7) What is Love? (1 Corinthians 13:7)
8) What are the roles and responsibilities of each person?
9) How often to have sex? What sexually pleases your mate?
10) Finding out that you are not to withhold sex from each other
   (1 Corinthians 7:3-4)
11) Having a blended family
12) Parenting styles and discipline
13) And many other issues

This is when you have to ask yourself, can you bear the weight of your mate's truth? This is when both people should be able to just be who they are, express their truth, and still receive love, acceptance, no judgement or abandonment; because a marriage is not about what FEELS good, what's COMFORTABLE and what's ACCEPTED BY SOCIETY. It's about *Matthew 19:6 AMP, "So they are no longer two, but one flesh. Therefore, what God has joined together, let no man separate" and (1 Corinthians 13:7 AMP) "Love bears all things [regardless of what comes], believes all things [looking for the best in each one], hopes all things [remaining steadfast during difficult times], endures all things [WITHOUT WEAKENING]. God gives us the grace to do it in marriage."*

This may be the time that you realize that good looks, sex and money alone will not sustain a marriage.

Don't be fooled by the natural, we have to operate in the spiritual to sustain a healthy marriage. It will take God, God, God, communication, understanding, respect, love, being honest about hard topics and working through the problems with Godly solutions. Trust God's word. *"But those who trust in the LORD will find new strength. They will soar high on wings like eagles; they will run and not grow weary; they shall walk and not faint." (Isaiah 40:31) "And we know [with great confidence] that God [who is deeply concerned about us] causes all things to work together [as a plan] for good for those who love God, to those who are called according to his plan and purpose. (Romans 8:28 AMP)*

Once you're married or if you're already married, you may want to have counseling every three months; just to stay calibrated on making decisions in your marriage that line up with God's word and not opinions or the voice of the dominate person in the marriage. Remember, God created marriage. So, we want our marriages to line up with his word and his will for our lives. Is marriage work? Absolutely; but it's SO WORTH IT! God promises in his word that it will be better in the end than it was in the beginning - *"Better is the end of a thing than it's beginning, and the patient in spirit is better than the proud in spirit. (Ecclesiastes 7:8KJV)*

If you thought he was God's gift to the world when you met him; God is saying that it will be So Much Better in the end.

Being a Wife... and a "Bonus Mom"

Mr. Right may have a child/children. Are you thinking "I didn't sign up for the child/children; I just signed up for him? Why do I have to get along with the child/children? If they don't like me, I won't like them or deal with them; after all, they are not mine...."

If you are thinking any of these things, then you will have to ask yourself if you're willing to be the lady and woman that you will need to be to have a blended family. In my experience, my Mr. Right has a daughter. Personally, I don't have any children yet. But, that doesn't change how I communicate and interact with her as my daughter. I treat her as if she's mine; because she is ours. Although I'm not her biological mother, she will never FEEL that I'm not. As you notice, I said that I am a "Bonus Mom" and not a Stepmother, because having me as a mom is a Bonus in her life, because I love her, cherish her and raise her, like she's my own. It's a bonus, to have another mother to love her the way I do. She has a wonderful and loving mother, but I just always want to make sure that she feels loved, cared for, and of value by me.

So, you may be wondering, "Was everything perfect the entire time, because if so; that's not the case for me?" The answer is no. Absolutely not. In the beginning, there were communication problems, unnecessary meanness, and confusion for our daughter on whether or not to like me, whether or not to communicate with me, what to call me, etc. To add to that, you have to remember; children that live outside of your home are being raised in a manner that is usually different than you would raise them (neither style is better or worse; just different).

There are habits and behaviors that children are used to at home that are a culture and environmental change, when they are in your home. There are things that you and your husband may or may not allow that is acceptable or unacceptable at their home. As you begin to unfold the layers of difference, communication in your eyes could become miscommunication or ineffective communication in their eyes. Structure in your eyes could be interpreted as mean or cruel. You could be giving love and getting nothing in return. While at the same time, your mate is saying and doing all of the right things; but at the end of the day, that hurt and pain is still there; simply because you care.

Always remember, your love can't stop at the sight of his children. My hope is to encourage you to continue to be loving, even when the child/children are not. Continue to love them, even when it hurts. Continue to love them, even when you're left out, lied on or misunderstood. God says, *"Let love and faithfulness never leave you; bind them around your neck, write them on the tablet of your heart." (Proverbs 3:3 NIV)*

Stand true to what's right in God's eyes, and he will always make sure that everything comes together for your good (Romans 8:28); because as long as you are consistently faithful God will crown you with the glory.

I'm Giving So Much, But Getting Nothing In Return

Have you ever felt like you were giving so much, but getting nothing in return? Well, there could be two things happening. Either your mate is truly not giving out anything (or giving very little) or your mate is giving you ALL THEY'VE GOT, with EVERYTHING in them; but you just can't see it. You may be thinking, "oh yeah, if he was giving

ANYTHING, I would be able to see it."

I hear these comments in marriages very often. Have you heard of the book *"The 5 Love Languages"* by Gary Chapman? It has changed marriages all over the world. It gives a real life perspective on the different ways of expressing love, and how each person desires to be loved. My husband and I took the quiz before we were engaged. We have the same primary love language and the same top three. Therefore, it's very easy for us to communicate our love to one another, because it's the same thing that each one of us wants to receive. Also, by having the psychology of why we do what we do, it makes it easier for us to be intentional and more effective when expressing our love to one another.

When anyone ever asks me for relationship advice, I always ask them, "Do you and your mate know each other's love language?" If not, I always tell them to take the quiz. Knowing this will help you both express love for one another in a way that the other can recognize and receive. This brings a higher level of fulfillment and love in a relationship. There are five different love languages expressed in Gary Chapman's book. The five languages are:

1) *Words of Affirmation* – verbal compliments that express your love and appreciation
2) *Acts of Service* – any act that eases the burden of responsibility
3) *Receiving Gifts* – tangible symbols that reflect your thoughtfulness and effort
4) *Quality Time* – focused and undivided attention spent together
5) *Physical Touch* – a non-sexual touch that reinforces your presence

For example: If your primary love language is quality time and your mate's primary love language is words of affirmation, a way that you could express your love for him would be to brag to others about him or write him love letters. A way that he could express his love for you is by turning off the cell phone and television, going for a walk, sitting in the park, planning date nights or starting a hobby together.

If there is a conflict in the relationship, you would need to speak to him

(A Words of Affirmation Person) words that build security and initiate a sincere apology. To you (A Quality Time Person), he would have to make eye contact, actively listen with empathy and not interrupt you. This is just scratching the surface of understanding and communicating love in an impactful and meaningful way to your mate. I HIGHLY recommend that you read it for yourself. It will totally bless your life, like it has for so many other relationships across the world.

What Do I Do, When It Seems Like NOTHING Is Working?

I want you to know that no matter what you're going through in your marriage and in your life; whether it's finances, children, communication, addictions, sex, in-laws, health, infidelity, disrespect, love, work, etc... no matter what it is, it's not too big for God! (John 16:33) There is nothing wrong with you or your life. You are not the only one going through it. God says, there is no problem new to man. There is nothing that we will go through, that someone else has not gone through AND come out Victorious!

The temptations in your life are no different from what others experience. And God is faithful. He will not allow the temptation to be more than YOU can stand. When you are tempted, he will show you a way out so that you can endure. (1 Corinthians 10:13 NLT)

KNOW that God promises us that he will never leave us or forsake us (1 Kings 8:57). Whatever trial, tribulation, affliction, storm or battle we may experience may be a surprise to us, but it's not a surprise to God. God says in his word, *"I have told you these things so that in me you may have PEACE. In this world you will have trouble. But take heart! I have overcome the world." (John 16:33 NIV)*

He created us in his own image (Ephesians 2:4); and we are MORE THAN CONQUERORS. We are more than enough. When we are at our weakest, we are actually at our strongest, BECAUSE God's Power (Strength) is made Perfect in weakness (2 Corinthians 12:9). He that is in us, is stronger than anything and everything in our life and the world.

"You are from God, little children, and have overcome them; because greater is He who is in you than he who is in the world." (1 John 4:4)

I know there are some pains that hurt so much, that could bring thoughts of violence and murder; but that's just the devil trying to come in, to steal, kill, and destroy your life. *The thief's purpose is to steal and kill and destroy. "My (God) purpose is to give them a rich and satisfying life." (John 10:10 NLT)*

In those moments you have to fight for your life. Pray for a breakthrough, like the mere air you breathe depends on it. Get in your closet and pray, scream, shout and cry out to the Lord. He will show up and show out in your life. God allows the unexpected circumstances to show up in our lives, so that he can show us how strong HE IS in getting us out of any storm.

"I have told you this, so that you might have peace in your hearts because of me. While you are in the world, you will have to suffer. But cheer up! I have defeated the world." (John 16:33 CEV)

When trials and tribulations come, God will show up and that's an opportunity for God to show you that no weapon formed against you shall prosper (Isaiah 54:17). We will never know how strong God is until we are under an attack; then God just brings us out on top. We have to see GOD'S POWER and his Covering in our problem. He will pull off a miracle if he chooses to bring his will to pass because he promises in his word, that his word will NEVER GO OUT AND COME BACK VOID (Isaiah 55:11). It will go out and do everything it was intended to do. Mastering marriage with God's Power, one storm at a time!

I pray that you reading my chapter has strengthened your faith in what God can and wants to do in your life and marriage, enlightened your thoughts, given you some practical things that could help you have success and victory in marriage, blessed your spirit and encouraged you to BE the Absolute Best Child of God, wife (helpmate) and Mother, God willed for you to be. God Bless You!

Sally J. Thompson, a native of Indianapolis, Indiana, is number nine of 13 children. With the love for God, and a clear understanding of her purpose in Christ, the Lord has allowed Sally to know that there are "no limits" to what God can or will do through her. She has a love for music, women, the youth and lost souls. As you listen to her minister in word and song, you will notice that she demonstrates openly a heart turned toward God and is proof that the hand of the Lord is upon her life.

God set Sally free from the guilt, shame, secrecy and depression caused by her abortion. She served as the Director of one of the Pregnancy Resource Centers in Indiana. God placed in her heart to speak to pastors to encourage them to speak about life and God's purpose for our lives, also to offer healing and forgiveness to men and women who have experienced abortion.

Sally has shared her testimony in magazines, on radio and television stations nationally and internationally including LeSea Broadcasting and TBN. Sally served on the Board of Director for the Life Centers Pregnancy Care Centers in Indianapolis, IN 2011 to 2015.

Sally married for the first time at the age of 45 years old in December 2014 to an awesome man of God, Minister, and Worship Leader Mr. Benjamin Thompson. Sally and her husband lives in Indianapolis, IN where they Pastor Progressive Life Ministries on the west side of Indianapolis.

Seeking To Be Made Whole Before Marriage

"Dear God, I desire a husband. Lord not my will
but your will be done."

This was the start of the last letter I wrote to God regarding my desire to be married. It's funny because out of the many letters that I've written to God about a husband, I never thought about God's will for my life or his plans for my marriage. I always told the Lord what I wanted in my husband: he needs to be tall, dark, handsome, rich, great job, nice car, big house and a nice bank account. My earlier letters were so materialistic and selfish on my part. My letters were all about what I needed him to be and nothing of what I could be to him. I didn't ask God for a husband that would love me or that he would have a heart for God. I remember one day when I was in prayer asking for a husband, the Lord said, "You're prepared for the wedding, but you're not prepared for marriage." Hmmm, I thought. What is the marriage, Lord why am I not ready for the marriage? I heard the Lord say, "Will you be made whole?" My prayers changed to, "Lord before I can get to him, Lord you get to me. Make me whole."

Ladies, the Lord wants us to get our house (His temple) in order. He wants us to take our position in life, and it may not be what you think it is. I pray, as you read this chapter, that you will ask God to open your heart to receive all that HE has in store for you. This chapter is for women who desire to be whole in Christ and want to become free from the things that are keeping us from doing God's will. Prompting those to be motivated to take a look at ourselves, and how we can be used to the fullest by the Lord. The Bible tells us to examine oneself. Search me oh God, what is it that's in me that's not like you? I pray that as you read this chapter you will feel God's anointing upon every page, that it will encourage and empower you to become whole in him.

Before going any further empty yourselves and come open to God. That he may feel you with a fresh Word and a fresh anointing. Renew our minds Lord to think like you. I want to be whole. I'm tired of struggling with the same issues. Teach me your ways. Show me "me" Lord, I want to be that virtuous woman, I want my home to be sanctified, I want to honor my husband as priest over our home, I want my children to rise and call me blessed, I want to be content in my singleness until you send me my husband. Lord I Thank You for Your Word that strengthens us to want to be more like you. Thank you in advance for what you're going to do in our lives through this chapter.

This chapter originated 10 years ago, by my own desire, to be whole in Christ Jesus. Yes, I am saved. Yes, He is Lord over my life, but something was still missing. I wanted and still craved the fulfillment of Christ. The instability and struggle was exhausting. Lord, I want to be made whole. How do I become complete in you?

CARRIERS OF LIFE

Ladies we were created to carry life both physically and spiritually. It's time for us to take our position in life so that our families can get in order. God created men to be the head of our homes and we have taken over, leaving our men misplaced. The things God has given us to carry are out of bounds because we are bound with the things of this world that we have picked up on our own. Our husbands, families, and our children are lost emotionally, in jails, on drugs, lacking in confidence and self-worth because we have neglected them. We don't have time to love and nurture them due to the many issues that we have neglected to deal with on our own like sexual abuse, abortion, molestation, abusive relationships both emotionally and physically. These issues lead us to depression and emotional instability if not dealt with.

"Therefore, we also, since we are surrounded by so great a cloud of witnesses, let us lay aside every weight, and the sin which so easily ensnares us, and let us run with endurance the race that is set before us, 2 looking unto Jesus, the author and finisher of our faith…" (Hebrews 12:1 NKJV)

It's time to take back what the enemy has stolen from us. Our joy, happiness, men, families, kids, neighborhoods, finances, and love for one another. God created women to be carriers. We must know who we are in Christ and our position in Christ that we may know our position in this world. Society is crippling, it tells us who we are supposed to be and what we are supposed to do. God created us, for His purposes. He has a plan already designed for us. We must look to His plans for our lives, His plans make us whole.

I met a guy that appeared to truly love the Lord. I was attracted to his love for Christ. As we began to talk and periodically see each other, I questioned the Lord, what is my position in this man's life? You know how single women can be? We meet a man, especially one that's after God's heart, and the first question that comes to mind is, "Lord is this my husband?" The Lord woke me up early one morning and told me that my position in this man's life was to pray for him, encourage him, and to be watchful over him in the spiritual realm, not stalk him, or to have sex with him. God told me that he did not choose me, God did this and it was an immense responsibility due to some things that the man would go through. He told me, although, I should feel honored to have this position, but it can be a dangerous position. He reminded me of how Eve lead Adam to the apple, and the destruction that followed for generations. Did Eve know her position? Ladies are we seeking to know our position in Christ, or are we seeking to see how we can get him to marry us? I found myself in Eve's shoes, knowing the Word that the Lord had spoken, but having then chosen to do my own thing instead by getting into a sexual relationship with this guy. Of course the relationship did not last.

I would like to encourage all women seeking to be married to become whole in Jesus Christ alone, first. Fall in love with Jesus, so you'll know what love is. You will know this when you're no longer seeking for a husband, only God's will for your life.

THE WOMAN WITH ISSUES

Guess what ladies, we all have physical and/or emotional issues. The Bible says that *"all have sinned, and come short of the glory of God." (Romans 3:23 NKJV)* The problem is how we handle our issues. We can learn a lot from the woman with the issue of blood.

Now a certain woman had a flow of blood for twelve years, and had suffered many things from many physicians. She had spent all that she had and was no better, but rather grew worse. When she heard about Jesus, she came behind Him in the crowd and touched His garment. For she said, *"If only I may touch His clothes, I shall be made well." (Mark 5:25 NKJV)*

What did the woman with the issue of blood have to do to get to Jesus? I could imagine that this woman was in so much pain, that she desperately dared to reach out to Jesus. She prayed her way through. She didn't send someone else to get him; but pressed her way through the crowd, utterly determined. Upon seeing the crowd she didn't run, therefore not allowing fear to stop her. She didn't give up on hope. She knew that if she could only get to Him, she would be made whole.

The woman with the issue of blood had to leave some things to get to Jesus. What and who are you willing to give up to become whole? She suffered for 12 years, no doubt she had tried many things on her own to find fulfillment but she continued looking until she found it in Christ Jesus. She heard about Jesus. Are we telling people about Jesus? You shouldn't assume that everyone knows Him. Do you know who Jesus is or do you just know about Him?

Do I believe that He is the way? Believing, I must decide in my mind that I don't care what I have to do, and that I will not give up until

I find Him. There's something that God wants to do in you. Lord I Surrender my mind, body and soul to you. Silver and gold I have none, but such as I have I give to you today Lord. It doesn't matter what you've been through, God wants to use you for His glory. Fix your eyes on Jesus and be determined to go all the way for Him. Ask God to teach you His ways. I want to be balanced. I want to love you, my husband and my family. *"Seek ye first the kingdom of God ... and all these things shall be added unto you."* (Matthew 6:33 KJV)

"Now a certain man was there who had an infirmity thirty-eight years. When Jesus saw him lying there, and knew that he already had been in that condition a long time, He said to him, 'Do you want to be made well?'" (John 5:5-6 NKJV)

Are you tired of suffering? Are you ready to give it to Jesus so you can be made whole?

"Jesus said to him, 'Rise, take up your bed and walk.' And immediately the man was made well, took up his bed, and walked." (John 5:8 NKJV)

The man had to do something. Are you ready to get up? Are you ready to deal with the issues that keep you bound? Jesus is telling us today to rise up out of that issue and let's be about our father's business. Immediately the man was made whole. He wants to do the same for you today. Right now you can become whole. Jesus Christ is waiting on you.

> *Jesus is telling us today to rise up out of that issue and let's be about our father's business.*

"Jesus says to the man, behold, thou art made whole; sin no more, lest a worse thing unto thee." (John 5:14 NKJV)

After the Lord delivers us, we can't go back into that same situation or it's going to be more difficult to come out the next time, if there is a next time.

"The man departed and told the Jews that it was Jesus which had made him whole." (John 5:15 NKJV)

When I was single I prayed often, Lord I want to be married. His response was always, my focus was off centered. God wants us to seek Him and for Him to be first in our lives. Don't get me wrong, there is nothing wrong with asking. His word tells us to ask and it shall be given, seek and you shall find. Seek who? Seeking Him and the right man will find you. We must want Jesus more than anything in our lives. Seek his ways. Ladies it's your time. What or who is holding you back from being made whole? Will you be made whole today?

"Search me, O God, and know my heart; Try me, and know my anxieties; And see if there is any wicked way in me, And lead me in the way everlasting." (Psalm 139:23-24 NKJV)

I began praying Lord make me whole. What is it that's in me that keeps me from doing your will? What is it that keeps me in fear? The Lord reminded me of the abortion I had in the past. My abortion was a secret to many. I knew that I was forgiven, but I didn't know that I needed to be set free. I was hanging on to guilt, regret, unforgiveness, and shame. I had a testimony that could save many babies still in the womb; to heal women who had experienced the same pain I experienced from abortion. The aftermath of my abortion resulted in depression. I didn't want to deal with it. I didn't want to talk about it. I was disgusted with myself. Ladies we are daily in emotional pain, numb to the reality of our condition. We walk around like nothing is wrong masking our deepest regrets. Wherever your pain may come from, a relationship that went bad, loss of a loved one, unaccomplished goals, pain from an abortion(s), physical or emotional (sexual) abuse or abandonment. God wants to heal you; He wants to make you whole. Hurting women are a menace to society. God has conditioned us to handle pain not for it to overtake us.

BROKEN

I was ready for change. I was broken and humble. I was open to whatever God wanted from me. In brokenness comes purification, and purification may be painful; but it is a must.
"Purge me with hyssop, and I shall be clean; Wash me, and I shall be

whiter than snow. Make me hear joy and gladness, That the bones You have broken may rejoice. Hide Your face from my sins, And blot out all my iniquities. Create in me a clean heart, O God, And renew a steadfast spirit within me." (Psalm 51:7-10 NKJV)

My prayer was: Lord take out everything in me that's not like you. I did not know the degree of devastation abortion had caused me. I did not seek God for direction when making the decision to abort. I did not consider the consequences. I did not seek good counsel.

I'M FREE

The woman who God has set free realizes who she is in Christ and guards her heart. Although she may experience life's ups and downs, she doesn't allow it to consume her being. She is free to be who God created her to be.

"Who may ascend into the hill of the Lord? Or who may stand in His holy place? He who has clean hands and a pure heart". (Psalms 24:3,4a NKJV)

The whole woman is free because God has set her free. The whole woman is a woman of virtue. She knows her purpose and destiny, because she seeks the Lord continually in prayer, fasting and meditating on the Word of God. She knows how to be still before the Lord, waiting to hear His voice. She may feel inadequate but she goes, because she knows God has called her and equipped her. She's a woman of integrity and knows her priorities and acts on them. She is balanced and knows her boundaries. She seeks wisdom from the Lord and receives the exceeding, abundantly, above all that she can ask. She has a good reputation in her communities because she is virtuous. She seeks to serve, esteeming others above herself. The whole woman is not perfect however she knows that the Lord will perfect those things which concern her.

No matter what age or challenging circumstances you've been through, it's not too late to be made whole; all it takes is a willing heart. Jesus asked the man "wilt thou be made whole?" (John 5:6

KJV) Women, let us too answer the call for us to be made whole. The broken woman can be restored and restoration only comes through Christ healing hand.

"Stand fast therefore in the liberty by which Christ has made us free, and do not be entangled again with a yoke of bondage." (Galatians 5:1 NKJV)

FOREVER GRATEFUL

"My soul, wait silently for God alone, For my expectation is from Him." (Psalm 62:5 NKJV)

The Lord answered my prayers! Had I known to seek God's will for my husband, perhaps I would have married long before the age of 45 years old. He was so right! I was prepared for the wedding, but I knew little about me nor what it means to be married. I'm so glad God lead me on the right path to being made whole before sending me my husband. In the process, I've learned (and still learning) many characteristics that's necessary to being a wife. I am learning how not to be selfish and to walk in humility. I am learning how to serve and to be content with where God has me, waiting for His direction. Most of all, I am learning the importance of loving me for who God created me to be. By the time I met my husband, I had already began walking in my purpose.

I realized that God had the perfect man for me. Oh and he is tall, dark, and handsome. He loves the Lord and he loves me and is wealthy in the Lord! While God was working on me, he was preparing my King. Four weeks after my last letter to God, I received a call from a friend I had known but had not spoken to in three years. Little did I know that call would lead to marriage. My husband came at a time I needed him most. It was God's will for him to be my husband. He had patience, compassion and loved to help serve with me for my mom. I will forever be grateful to God for sending Benjamin Thompson into my life. I'm grateful to the Lord that I can openly talk to my husband and share with him all that God has brought me through to be whole. Now we are poised for the next chapter in our lives.

Adrienne Y. Wharton is the Founder, CEO of I Luv ♥ My Hubby. She is passionate about giving wives the tools to develop a deeper relationship with their husbands and an unwavering faith to succeed in marriage. She is dedicated to dispelling the myth that marriage is disposable and divorce should not be an option. Adrienne believes that with God, couples can WIN in marriage. She is an entrepreneur, social worker, dream builder, author and COO of Brother Pass it On, Inc., where she and her hubby minister outside the walls of the church.

Adrienne was born in Springfield, TN and raised in Indianapolis, IN. She and her family lived in Atlanta for 17 years before God called them to return home to Indianapolis five years ago. She has been married to Mychal Wharton for 19 years and is the mother of Mychal-Nichelle and Zion Wharton.

Adrienne holds a B.A. degree in Criminal Justice from Clark-Atlanta University. She worked as a juvenile probation officer for over 10 years, and then worked in non-profit housing moving families into home ownership.

Adrienne's passion is not only helping wives, but also helping others discover and develop their dreams to turn it into entrepreneurship. Adrienne believes God gives everyone a purpose and wants everyone to walk in that purpose. "The purposes of a person's heart are deep waters, but one who has insight draws them out" (Proverbs 20:5, NIV). She believes that when you walk in your purpose, your life changes forever. Most people never step into their greatness because of fear. One of her favorite quotes is "Fear is one of the biggest dream killers there is. Don't live a life of regrets because fear held you back from your dreams." Adrienne stands on and reminds everyone of Timothy 1:7 (AMP), "For God did not give us a spirit of timidity or cowardice or fear, but [He has given us a spirit] of power and of love and of sound judgment and personal discipline [abilities that result in a calm, well-balanced mind and self-control]."

Worthy to Be Loved... I Love My Hubby

"Where's my Daddy?"

Every summer I would fly to Tennessee to visit my father. I was able to tell my friends about all the fun and exciting experiences I had when I returned to school from summer vacation. However, this particular summer changed my life. I remember those words that were spoken to me that cut like a knife. Words that twisted, turned, and mangled part of my spirit and soul. I was putting the finishing touches to my hair with a white yarn ribbon around my ponytail. I had on a white shirt with the brown cowboy vest and gauchos to match. I thought I was sharp as a tack.

I walked down the hall to the family room where my father was sitting with his friend. I looked at my dad to show off my outfit. Then the words came out of his friend's mouth, like a hunter firing his arrow as it pierces through the air and striking his prey, "You are so ugly." That arrow struck deep and ripped down my soul from top to bottom. My aunt yelled and scolded the friend at the words he had spoken to me. However, my father sat there drunk and just said, "Man shut up." "Shut up" was not the response I was looking for in order to take the arrow out. My father didn't come to my defense, his only child. At eight years old, this catastrophic event was another turning point that started the cycle of self-hate about my looks, how I spoke, the answers I gave, and how I wanted others to view me. My feelings about people, especially men, became hardened forever. A feeling that an eight-year-old should not have to endure throughout life.

"From Ugly to the Abuse"

The flight back to Indianapolis was not pleasant. My mind kept flashing back to the moment that a grown man called me "ugly.". That experience made me more aware of people's comments about me, the actions of others and my reactions in certain situations. It always made me more aware of what was going on at home. My mom began dating "Wood" when I was about four years old. I remember he had several businesses and played professional football for a short while. I remember they would argue, but it didn't bother me because I spent a majority of the time with my grandparents at their home. That fall I remember my mom moved us to a new apartment in the city closer to my grandparent's home. I called our new home the "house of horror."

This was a pivotal moment in my life when things went from bad to worse. The arguments between my mom and Wood got worse. I begin remembering things about their past arguments. Since my return from Tennessee I became aware that Wood would get irritated over simple things. He would argue with my mom if we didn't get home at a certain time, why my mom wore a particular outfit, even who she was talking to on the phone. Often times, if the arguments escalated he would leave the apartment only to return with more anger. If my mom would not let him in the apartment building he would just hold the buzzer to our apartment and it would continuously ring. He would use this tactic often thinking she would get so tired of the noise that she would eventually let him upstairs; unfortunately, most of the time it worked. During one of the many mad moments at the house of horror Wood buzzed all the residents until someone let him in the building. He came upstairs to the third floor and begin banging on the door. He caused so much ruckus that the neighbors came out to see what was going on.

All of his cursing and fussing caused her to give in to his behavior.

Also, she was concerned that our neighbors would complain to management and she had sheer embarrassment. During one particular argument, he began yelling and screaming at my mother. She moved from room to room to try to get away from him. They ended up in the hallway directly in front of my bedroom. I heard Wood asking her questions like, "Why was he talking to you?", "What were you doing over there?", "Why did you have that dress on?" I remember thinking "What and who is he talking about?" I came out of my bedroom, but I didn't say a word. My mom was crying and telling me to go back in my bedroom, but I couldn't move. I was frozen standing in the entryway near the front door. The movement of their bodies was so surreal; it was like everything was in slow motion. Wood's frame was 6'3, 250lbs, with huge hands and feet of a giant. I remember him pulling his arm back like he was getting ready to swing a bat. He moved it forward as if he was going to hit the ball, and when he did the ball was my mother's face. He hit her until blood was running down her face. He pushed and pulled on her body, like a limp Raggedy Ann doll, then just left the apartment.

"Learning to Pray"

Living with my grandparents was a blessing and a safe haven. My grandmother Susie, who everyone called "Grannie," had a beautiful spirit. She taught me how to pray, how to cook, and how to clean. She was a prayer warrior. Everyone would call "Grannie" for prayer. At bedtime, I would kneel on the side of the bed and listen to her prayer for everyone, even those in my mind like Wood, that didn't deserve her prayer. I attended church between both of my grandparents. My grandmother was a member of the Apostolic domination and my grandfather was of the Methodist Episcopal domination, African Methodist Episcopal, to be exact. Being taught the foundation of both religions, I was able to intertwine both in my life as I got older. This was fundamental to me as a teenager and young adult. Listening to her prayers as a child I began to mimic them until I was able to turn them into my personal prayers, prayers that I needed God to hear from me. Just like my grandmother, I began to pray for my enemies knowing one day they would be my footstool (Psalm 110:1 NLT).

"Dark Skinned and Gap Tooth"

Through the years the arguments between my mother and Wood would continue, as well as going down to Tennessee to see my dad for the summer. I remember kids "jonning" a term, meaning to talk about someone bad for something they had, didn't have, or their looks. I absolutely hated that game. First because I wasn't good at it, second because they were talking about the areas I was most sensitive about and third I didn't have tough skin to let it roll off my back and move on. Instead I would go home and cry. During my preteen and teen years, I was called "dark" or told I wasn't "cute" like my friends whose melanin was on the lighter side. I also felt uncomfortable about the gap between my front teeth, which I inherited from my father. The words I heard about myself as a child I couldn't get pass. Plus, the insults that were hurtled towards me as a teenager didn't help the poor self-image I had about myself. Although, my mother, grandmother, aunt and family would tell me how beautiful I was, it's different when it comes from your friends and boys.

"Puppy Love"

When I turned fifteen, I meet a young man in Tennessee who was much older and thought I was in love. He told me all the things I wanted and needed to hear. He told me I was beautiful and loved everything about me that I didn't like. I enjoyed hanging out with him and all my friends. I was the center of attention since I wasn't from that small town, but from up North. When I returned home he would call me all the time reinforcing all the things that I needed to hear between all the arguing and fighting at home. One day my mom picked up the phone and was angry after hearing our conversation and my "boyfriend" expressing his love for me. This became of source of contention between us. I felt she could not tell me anything because of the things I saw between her and Wood. I felt she was the last person on earth to tell me about love. Needing to feel the sense of love and security, I became very rebellious. That rebellion turned into something as a teenager I really was not ready to handle. My last summer in Tennessee I became pregnant. Reality hit me hard and I didn't know what to do. My boyfriend wanted me to move to Tennessee and be a family with him. I was so confused. I didn't know the first thing about being a mother because I was still a child. I prayed like my grandmother taught me. I prayed and prayed and prayed. I finally made the decision to not have the child. I was a child myself and by the grace of God I was able to move forward. The puppy love ended and I only had memories. The memories of that time in my life that would eventually fade into the abyss.

"A Change is Coming"

As I begin to mature and develop from a teenager to young adult, I learned to embrace my beauty. I became heavily involved in church. I travelled all over the country with the YPD, Young People's Department, of the AME church. I met people and formed friendships that have lasted 30 plus years. This new group of people helped me to feel better about myself. The resources, guidance and training gave me opportunities for leadership experiences in church and society. I felt a change within me. I saw things differently and grew closer to God during this time. I also went off to college at Clark Atlanta University where I continued to serve in the YPD and became a leader on my campus. This was a wonderful time in my life. I began dating; however, I was very standoffish with guys. I was told "you are too hard to get next to," "you're mean," and "my attitude was bad." However, to me I just didn't take any mess from guys and if you did something I didn't like it was over! I didn't give guys much of a chance because of what I saw growing up and my past experiences.

"Always the Bridesmaid Never the Bride"

After college, I came back home to Indianapolis for a short while. All of my friends were getting married. I dated, but never found "the one." At one point I thought I had, but God had the best waiting for me. This relationship was again one with an older guy that I thought was good for me. He provided for me all the "words" I needed to make me feel good about myself. I thought we would get married one day. During this relationship, several of my friends got married;

at one point, I had six bridesmaids' dresses in my closet. I was like really, when will it be my turn. There were several things that were obvious that I knew were not good in this relationship, but I turned a blind eye because I wanted to be a bride.

The things I had prided myself on as a woman not to take from a man, I slowly began to let fall to the wayside. This heavy feeling of depression fell on me, something I had never experienced. I begin to pray asking God to give me comfort and understanding. One evening I had a dream and God gave me a CLEAR message. I dreamt I had on a beautiful wedding gown and the church was full of people. I walked down the aisle and when the minister asked if I accepted his hand in marriage I said "NO"! Not a sad no, but a stern, no nonsense, adamant NO! I woke up and knew he was not the one. Of course, things didn't end well; however, I was confident with my choice. I remember falling to my knees and asking God to take away my desire to be in a relationship and when He sent me my Boaz, I would be open and ready. From that point forward I attended church regularly, bible study and immersed myself in things I enjoyed. God and I had long conversations and I never had that desire to be in a relationship. It was just me and the Lord. I was the happiest I had been in a long time.

"My Boaz"

During the fall of 1996 I met a young lady at a work training session. We became friends instantly. She had just recently gotten married and her husband was a very nice guy. We would hang out from time to time and talked constantly. One day she told me she wanted to introduce me to a guy that would be absolutely perfect for me. She attended college with him at Central State University. I didn't give the statement much thought. However, she was crystal clear that when she introduced us she didn't want either of us to be dating. She would tell me when she saw him out, but it very seldom. She finally gave me his phone number in March of 1998 and told me to invite him to my birthday party. I called, but had to leave a message inviting a total stranger to my birthday party, and he didn't even show up. He called me about a week later. During that time, I was working 2p-12a and my days off rotated. I will never forget Rev. Frank Madison Reid III from Bethel AME church in Baltimore was in Indianapolis for revival. When Mychal called me, I had only been home for about an hour from revival. My spirit was filled with the words Rev. Reid had spoken.

Of course, when you first talk to someone you do the formal introductions and ask about family, siblings, school etc. We got all of the preliminaries out of the way, and then Mychal asked me, "What did you do today?" That was the beginning of my life with him. I told him about Rev. Reid's message and we talked until 2am. Each night he would call me and we would have a conversation about Rev. Reid's message from the evening. Our conversations were so free flowing, no pretenses, just old fashion conversation. Mychal finally asked me out, however I could only do lunch because of my rotating work schedule. We settled on a lunch date for March 27th. The plan was to meet him at his job and we would walk together to the restaurant. I was really interested in this guy. I told my best friend about him and what a small world - she was his co-worker. She told me that I was going to really like him and then she described him to me. "He has a light complexion with green eyes." Immediately those feelings of insecurity of the little black ugly girl with the gap in her teeth began to take over my mind. I prayed to get my feelings under control and to remember what the scripture tells me about myself, "I am fearfully and wonderfully made" Psalms139:14. We met; we ate; we talked; we met later, and we have never gone without seeing or talking to each other from that day forward. All those insecurities that were inside of me began to fade away. God gave me a sense of peace when Mychal told me I was beautiful…it was genuine, that he loved my dark skin…it was from his heart, and the gap in my teeth was just another part of beauty. God had sent me my Boaz. Our meeting was so unexpected and the thought of being in a relationship was somewhere in the far away distance for me. As our relationship developed and this new love blossomed, Mychal asked me to marry him in July, 1998. I have always been a praying person so I prayed and asked God to reveal to me how I should proceed. God gave me the green light. We were married March 27, 1999.

"Real Love"

We married and three weeks later we moved to Atlanta. We were newlyweds in uncharted waters without a compass. We only had each other and God to rely on. Neither one of us saw strong marriages when we were growing up and the marriages we did see were not what we wanted for ours. Being alone in a city without any family support will make or break a relationship. As the saying goes, "Only the strong will survive." Throughout our almost 20 years together we have gone through our trials and tribulations. We learned how to be a strong married couple with the help of God. At times Satan would attack me, especially when we had a disagreement. Those words "you're ugly," would creep up in my head, or the darkness of my skin became a concern. I had told Mychal about my past and all the hurt I felt. I would ask him "why" questions: "Why do you love me?" "Why do you love my dark skin?" I needed answers to all of the "why" questions to all of the insecurities I had about myself. He stopped me in my tracks and looked me in what he says are my beautiful brown doe eyes and said, "Before I leave this earth you will know what REAL LOVE is." "He who finds a wife finds what is good" (Proverbs 18:22 CEB). I can say without a doubt that's why I love my hubby!

> *We were newlyweds in uncharted waters without a compass.*

Renee Lacey Wharton desires to be a woman after God's own heart. She desires to help hurting women free the little girl inside and live the abundant life God has designed for them, by sharing her personal testimony of God's protection and grace.

Born and raised in Indianapolis, Indiana, Renee is a graduate of Broad Ripple High School. Her heart for women led to a lengthy career as a self-employed Cosmetologist where she enjoyed over 18 years of helping women look and feel their confident best. During her years as a Cosmetologist, Renee prided herself on running her business as efficiently as possible. After retiring from cosmetology, Renee's passion for efficiency and organization led her to pursue a degree in Business Management from Indiana Wesleyan University where she graduated Summa Cum Laude. She went on to receive a Master's Degree in Strategic Leadership and Design from the University of Indianapolis. She now enjoys a career in the Energy Industry where she is actively involved in Women's Empowerment efforts.

Renee and her husband Brian have been married for 23 years and have three sons, Brandon, Bryce and Brentton. She is thankful for the balance and joy her family brings to her life.

Renee has a passion for worship and is actively involved in the worship ministry at her church. She has previously served alongside her husband as a Marriage Ministry Facilitator and sincerely desires to build strong, prosperous marriages for the kingdom of God.

Safe In His Arms

Sitting on the edge of my bed, tears streaming down my face, I questioned the decision I made to marry the only man, besides my grandfather, who had ever made me feel secure. As I sat holding the brochure that outlined all the amenities of the complex I had chosen to be my next home, if I decided to go through with the move, I carefully contemplated what I should do. Still remembering our first hug, I vividly recalled my earliest encounter with feelings of being covered, protected and safe; all feelings that escaped me at this very moment.

My entire life had been one blunder after another with lots of interruptions and feelings of simply being in the way. As a child, I often felt like a burden rather than a blessing and didn't even know that I was worthy of love. Holding onto the hope that I would feel that blanket of security I experienced from our first embrace, I sat in silence contemplating what just might be the best or possibly the worst decision of my life thus far. I didn't want to give up on my marriage. I couldn't, however, help but wonder if I had made the wrong choice in a partner. I wanted to be happy and, as I considered the time each of us spent in silence and the conversations that weren't being had, happiness seemed so far away. But my pride wouldn't let me quit. The thought of what divorce would do to my children wouldn't let me quit. The thought of starting over and finding yet another inadequate love wouldn't let me quit. I had to succeed at something and since nothing else in life had rendered victory I needed to call this marriage a win, even if I was miserable.

For what seemed like forever, feelings of safety and protection had evaded me. Now years into our marriage, I still longed for those feelings and couldn't completely understand why I could never seem to take hold of them. In addition to feeling uncovered, I had feelings of resentment and anger toward my husband. Most importantly, the pain of feeling unloved was too much to bear. I had to honestly admit that I didn't actually know what love really looked like. When I thought of love, images of broken homes and unforgiving families crowded my mind. I had experienced great rejection in life and had not experienced love that didn't include emotional pain. As a result, my ability to compare was limited. I honestly wondered if this was as good as it gets; if this was what love was supposed to be for me. After all, it was all I had known. No matter how much time had passed, I couldn't shake this feeling of being unworthy of love, and with each passing day I longed to understand it. I refused to believe that love was only a fairy tale. Love had to be more than just a feeling or desire and I held on to the hope that I would one day experience it in its fullest form.

Roots Run Deep

As a young woman, I was so happy to find someone who accepted me, seemingly unconditionally, that I didn't recognize the damage that had already been done to my heart. My constant cries to God had gone unanswered, but at this moment I was desperate. I was determined to find what I needed, even if it meant being still and letting God clearly instruct on my next move. Over the next several months, as I continuously begged God to know true love, He waited patiently for me to come to Him unselfishly asking for His understanding of love rather than the preconceived notion I had been chasing. During that time, I didn't pray for my marriage. I had given up on that. Instead, I prayed for an understanding of my life and all that was missing. I prayed to understand why I had been alienated from love and hadn't experienced it as others had. The more I prayed, the more I longed for it. The more I prayed, the more God unlocked my heart to receive it.

As God deepened my understanding of these feelings of being unworthy of love, I grew to understand the root of my pain. My feelings developed as a result of wounds that were far deeper than the eye could see. Those wounds had been present for many years and had nothing to do with my husband. They had everything to do with the painful childhood that I had buried and vowed not to allow to affect my life. Yet, my life had been affected more than I cared to admit. As I considered the wounds I carried into the marriage, I recognized wounds my husband carried into the marriage as well. I then recognized how those wounds dictated the relationship we had with one another and stifled our marriage. Both of us were so focused on what we hadn't received from those whom we thought should have loved us unconditionally, that we weren't able to love one another the way God had intended.

> *As God deepened my understanding of these feelings of being unworthy of love, I grew to understand the root of my pain.*

It wasn't until I earnestly prayed to God about all that I was experiencing that He began to loose the shackles that had kept me bound for far too long. The Bible tells us that, *"When you bow down before the Lord and admit your dependence on him, he will lift you up and give you honor." (James 4:10 NLT)* In my earnest plea for love, God showed me my heart and where all these feelings of resentment and anger were truly coming from. Once God opened my eyes to my own feelings of inadequacy and unworthiness, I could truly examine the motivations within my marriage. When I finally decided to offer it all to God rather than working out what I could on my own and then begging God to do the rest, the sadness I was experiencing began to lift.

During my quiet times with God, as I understood my own plight more and more, I felt compelled to pray for my marriage. As I prayed for guidance on what to do next, God specifically told me that he had created me a free will being and that I had the power to choose whether to stay or go. He gently whispered, "You can go, but that is not what I have for you." He made it plainly clear that His plan was never for me to walk away from my marriage because of the pain that I was feeling. Instead, He wanted to draw me closer to Him. As a result of my earnest cries for understanding, God had taken my desire to be loved and turned it into an unquenchable thirst for more of Him. The more I turned my heart over to God, the more I saw His hand shaping and molding me in the darkest moments of my life; even during the darkest moments within my marriage.

Love and Acceptance

Understanding the degree to which God loves us is the key to being free from the stronghold of insecurity and feelings of being unworthy of love. That first hug between me and my husband was merely a glimpse into the love and security God wanted to provide. Although I confessed God as my heavenly father, I had not experienced a father's love in a way that allowed me to take the limits off of God's love for me. My despairing cries to know love as God intends eventually taught me to receive love in this way. Ephesians 3:18 explains, *"And may you have the power to understand, as all God's people should, how wide, how long, how high, and how deep his love is." (NLT)* I had never known love so deep and without pain. I had heard about this amazing love my entire life, but had never truly experienced it for myself. I had to learn what it meant to unreservedly and wholeheartedly accept God's love. Doing so allowed me the freedom to experience an earthly revelation of love as well.

Totally accepting God's infinite love for me, opened my heart to recognize the simple ways in which my husband displayed love for me. It also caused me to learn more about our love than I had in the past. I learned to allow our love to be as unique as God had created it to be. In doing so, I recognized that our love was ours; simple and unrefined. It was not what I had seen couples put on display, and it was not the fairy tale images I had allowed to consume the desires within me. I had to learn not to compare our love to what I thought I knew about other relationships and then expect to see it blossom into all that God desired for it to be. I had to accept our love in its totality; the good, the not so good, the successes and the failures. Then and only then would I see our marriage as God had designed.

A Change in Perspectives

During my reflection, I came to understand that God never said our mates would be perfect. In fact, I believe His only desire is that our mates help draw us closer to Him. Sometimes that drawing will come from struggle and disappointment. As Christians, we often believe that our mate's maturity, holiness and strength are the things that draw us not only to them, but also to God. When, in fact, it is actually those areas of weakness that God uses to cultivate us as living sacrifices unto Him. It is often our spouse's weaknesses that drive us to our knees and have a great impact on our walk with Christ.

For years, I had convinced myself that what I needed in the area of love, my husband was unable to provide. In my eyes, his weaknesses disqualified him from truly loving me as I needed to be loved. His weaknesses, magnified by my insecurity, made the marriage unbearable. Initially, I thought marriage would give me what I needed in the area of love. Never did I consider that my insecurity would only heighten the degree to which I felt unworthy of love. I didn't realize what I was seeking could only come from God. Yet this unrelenting desire to know love led me right to Him. Psalm 37:4 *(NLT)* tells us that if *"we delight ourselves in the Lord, He will give us the desires of our heart."* My heart desired something that could only come from God. When I truly turned my desire over to God, He removed the scales from my eyes and allowed me to see love as He desires it for me. I was then able to receive pure love from my husband regardless of his flaws.

Allowing God to transform my thoughts caused me to see our marriage in a different light. Rather than see our differences and insecurities as hindrances, I am now able to see them, embrace them, and look for ways to strengthen our relationship as a result of them. While I have always had my own desires to grow deeper in my understanding of God, I have to admit that I never previously considered what that meant for my husband. He, too, has areas that he desires for God to touch; areas that are not perfect and in need of repair. Although our areas may be different, they are equally important to each of us. Just as I had to allow God to pull back the layers of my heart, I also have to give my husband the space he needs to allow God into those areas he desires to see changed. I must allow him room to develop in his gifts as much as I need and want room to do the same.

For years, our marriage suffered because of my inability to embrace the love that God had for me. Looking back and reflecting on times when love was uncertain, I can now see how I used my insecurity to make excuses rather than using it to build a strong foundation within our marriage. I was so focused on what I felt my husband was not equipped to give me that I used his weaknesses as an excuse not to deepen my own relationship with God. I had proven God faithful in so many other areas of my life, but had not allowed Him to pull back the layers of my heart so that I could experience the fullness of His love.

Healing of the Heart

Allowing God to heal this broken place opened up my heart to experience the love I so desired from my husband. As my heart healed, our marriage healed. The more I see myself, the more I see my husband as God sees him. The more I heal, the more I open up and allow God to do the work in our marriage that He has always intended to do. The more I grow, the more in love I fall with the man that originally captured my heart. The more I find God's grace, the more grace I exhibit to my husband and allow him to be who God is grooming him to be. During my journey of self-discovery, God revealed that I had been so focused on my husband's flaws that I couldn't see what he is to me. I couldn't see how necessary he is to my own development. I didn't understand the essential connection we have and its necessity for fulfilling God's purpose. I now understand that connection and how God strategically placed us in each other's lives. As a result of this understanding, my respect and admiration for my husband has completely changed. I have an entirely new appreciation for him and his role in my life. This understanding has broken the cycle of pain and resentment in our marriage and I once again feel the security I felt during our first embrace.

For far too long we tried to conquer marriage on our own terms instead of completely turning it over to God. Within our marriage, every vow has been tested and, although God never promised there wouldn't be seasons of more worse than better, He did promise *"... that God, who began the good work within you, will continue His work until it is finally finished on the day when Christ Jesus returns."* *(Philippians 1:6 NLT)* Our relationship has been tried. It has been broken and rebuilt. We are now able to look back at the bitterness of the breaking and see the beauty of the struggle. Every moment was necessary to build our relationship to the point that allows us to openly and honestly love one another. We no longer allow our flaws to rule in our marriage, but rather understand that those flaws assist in our growth and we embrace the journey, TOGETHER.

The decision to stay and let God do the work that He had always wanted to do was the best decision I could have made at that moment. Allowing God to till the soil of my heart removed years of anguish and pain that had not only eroded the love in my marriage, but that had also crippled me in so many other ways. The decision to stay and dig deep inside to find the reason behind the feelings opened a whole new world for us. I not only grew in my personal walk with God, but our marriage continues to grow with each passing day. And just as God promised, the years have been restored.

If you find yourself questioning love and wondering if your marriage is meant to be, I challenge you to seek God and find out what He is really trying to reveal. Find that deep rooted seed that He is trying to dig up. Your marriage CAN work and it just may be the breeding ground for healing and breakthrough that can only happen with God's grace. James 1:3 and 4 tells us, *"For you know that when your faith is tested, your endurance has a chance to grow. So let it grow, for when your endurance is fully developed, you will be perfect and complete, needing nothing."* *(NLT)* God desires for each of us to be whole. Although many of us may still be broken while in our marriages, God can use marriage as a healing place for His glory if we allow Him into those areas of brokenness and insecurity. I pray that you earnestly take your concerns to God and allow Him to cultivate within you what is necessary for your growth. I pray that His grace would find you and pull back the layers of your heart. I pray that it finds you in your darkest moments and that He showers you with understanding of just how vast His love is for you. I pray that you take off that blanket of insecurity so that you, too, can feel safe in His arms.

LaTasha C. White was called to elevate in her life's ministry as she gave God her "yes" to serve women in the area of self leadership. In addition to being a registered nurse, she saw fit to sharpen her call and become a Certified Leadership Coach through the John Maxwell Team and Human Behavior Consultant with Authentic Identity Institute. In early 2016, she and her husband launched Grow Into Victory Intentionally, LLC. At GIVIN, they specialize in self leadership coaching through His R.I.B., an Elite Wives Online Academy, virtual mastermind groups, one on one coaching, DISC personality assessments and spiritual gift analysis.

LaTasha has had the honor of being a 2-time published author with Authentic Identity Institute's Publishing Division. In A Glimpse of Glory-Seeing God in the Midst of it all, 2017, she writes of the transparent journey of her 20-year marriage to husband, Reginald. She openly shares her life, so that she may not only be a testimony, but also a light for others who need to be lead to the throne. Her second published work in Positioned to Prosper, also 2017, with AIC she wants you to know your beginning doesn't define your ending.

LaTasha has been married 21 years to Reginald. They are the proud parents of 2 young men, Omar, 16, Zharquan, 20, and a 24-year-old daughter, Kiara, the mother of their grandson, 3-year-old Kamari.

$\mathcal{A}$re You His Rib or Just the Scar?

"Then the Lord God made a woman from the rib he had taken out of the man, and he brought her to the man. The man said, 'This is now bone of my bones and flesh of my flesh; she shall be called 'woman', and for she was taken out of a man.'" (Genesis 2:22 NIV)

This scripture was God's intention, my behavior proved it was not mine, at all! If honor and respect were the requirements to be the rib of the man God chose for me, I was not fit.

In the following pages, I will share my heart with you on how I walked through learning to become my husband's rib, and finally being worthy of the mandate I was given by God to be his wife. It sounds great to get married, but do we understand what that really means before we do it?

The Calm Before the Storm

I was blissfully happy. I had a job, a car, an apartment, and now a husband who adored me. Why did I need conflict and turmoil where there was none?

Becoming a bride at 19 years old, only 11 months after first laying eyes on the man who would make me his bride, presents its own set of challenges that we had coming a mile away now. I was an "old soul" for my age, yet I had so much growing up to do.

I had no understanding or teaching of what it meant to be a wife, much less my husband's rib. My parents divorced when I was just 5 years old. My dad was around, but I missed out on the part where you get to see your parents interact as a couple. My grandparents were married for over 50 years. They were the definition of a traditional marriage, where you work hard and provide for your family, but there was not a lot of talk of how to work through issues as a couple, or how you make decisions, or live life together. I knew I loved my fiancée, and that I could figure out how to make it work.

I'd jumped headfirst into being a wife, and it was easy at first, because my husband never told me "no" to anything. If I wanted it, he'd figure out how I could have it. Well this is great. If married life is having a husband who sees to it that you're happy, at all times, I'll take it! I would tell him over and over, "you don't have to do all of these things for me." He'd continually buy me things and later I found out that this was his idea of how to keep a woman. We both had a lot to learn. But, who would teach us, except mistakes and time?

The Winds Are Picking Up

Fast forward just four years, reality set in. My father had passed away. We'd started our family. Quickly I had to realize it wasn't about me anymore, and had to grow up and learn what was really important in life. We were faced with the unthinkable. My husband had fallen very sick, very quickly, and very unexpectedly. No doctors could give answers. We were faced with the choice to band together, take ownership of our vows, and understand that the "for sickness and in health" was happening. What do we do now? Our faith increased, as we felt our only option was to pray and trust that God knew better than we did, and was in control of all. I had to step up and grow up, fill in where my husband was no longer able.

There was a lot of heartache and hard feelings that I was harboring from past relationships and even the broken relationship with my father, that I projected so much of it on my husband. I did know enough to know I didn't want divorce as an option, but that didn't keep me from bringing it up at the first sign of an argument or disagreement, for years!

Who was I to treat him so terribly? I lived in the lane of "I'll always get you before you get me." It was my protection mechanism, and I'd vowed to not be broken by a man again. I learned years later that my husband almost expected this, as he was raised by a very stern mother. It was no surprise to him that I would speak this way. I realize now that there were so many times that I cut him down with words like a knife to the jugular. I'd scream and yell, about anything. It's embarrassing to recall now. He was very quick tempered back then, and I knew how to push his buttons, and I would go for the gut. Anytime, I felt like he hurt me or spoke to me in a disrespectful way, I'd make it my business to make him feel how he'd made me feel.

Pressure Is Building

The center of a hurricane is warmer than its surroundings, and forms under weak high-altitude winds. The main energy source is the heat. Wow! That definitely described our marriage perfectly at the time. Days would go by without speaking. Nights would grow colder and more silent, senseless bickering when words did exchange. I went to all the wrong people to "vent," which only ended up with bad advice and a worsening home life. Not one of those people I'd gone to for help directed me to prayer and the Word.

Hindsight lesson: Always seek wisdom vs. advice. If a person has not been through what you are going through, they cannot give wisdom. They can only give advice; choose wisely whose advice you take. Not everyone has your best interest in mind when they advise you. The saddest part is they may have deep seated issues that prevent them from being able to be happy for you, but they may not be aware. When you share with someone, be sure they have the capacity to handle what you are requesting of them.

The Eye of the Hurricane

In the eye of our life's hurricane, we fought many battles, some of which we created by our own mismanagement of our blessings, and others we felt like came out of nowhere. Hands down, if we had to pinpoint one area that challenged us the most, it would've been when we realized life would forever change, and we had to make some tough decisions.

By God's grace and my newly found faith, at that time, my decision was quick and not up for debate in my mind. Whatever I needed to do to help my husband cope with the diagnosis he'd been given to live the rest of his life on dialysis, as he is not a transplant candidate, I was going to do. That decision is one of few that I would not redo, take back, or change. Somehow in that moment I knew that my vows were a covenant not to be broken, and that I was to rise up and become the rib I was called to be. Continually, he has been bombarded with a number of health issues that aren't ever a quick answer. We have become really good at our battle plan of attack. Prayer changes everything. The picture of health on the exterior does not match the web of destruction on the inside of his body.

> *Somehow in that moment I knew that my vows were a covenant not to be broken, and that I was to rise up and become the rib I was called to be.*

The part we have loved is how God continues to show up and spare hubby's life when the doctors seem to not have an answer as to what happened to the nodules we were going to biopsy or why have his numbers improved without intervention to how has he lived so well for so long? He is definitely a living testimony, that God has graced me to witness. In many ways, I have to be grateful for the challenges, although they are many, and we do get tired. You see, the original symptoms of his quickly failing health started in the year 2000; it is now 2018 and we are still in the "for better for worse, in sickness and health battle."

Every single day with the sinking of each needle and the churning of the machine to clean my husband's toxic blood, your mind wanders and you begin to wonder "what if?" How long can this sustain life? Do I push past the current circumstance to the uncertain future? Do I let what the devil meant for bad rob me of my good? Why should I encourage him to be more and to do more? We should get a pass on all of the extra stuff because there is already so much to deal with. WRONG!

Hindsight lesson: God gives his greatest tests to those who can withstand the storms and come out better on the other side. Our lives are a testimony to help the next person know that they too can push through. There may not be an end, but there is a sustaining grace that allows us to stand against the winds together, and fight with all we have to give God the victory over the circumstance. The very fact that you are reading this story is a testament to the faith and resolve we have to help others through the side of marriage that isn't fun and games and surely doesn't smell like roses.

The Aftermath: Destruction or Reconstruction

So the question became, more destruction or do we figure out how to reconstruct what's been torn down and damaged? This happens to be our reality, but it's no different than whatever storms you and your spouse weather. We always have a choice. How you choose determines your victory or demise. We chose to have victory and understand that the tests only strengthen our testimony. Sure, we have had and continue to have times that we get a little discouraged with it all, but the alternative is we still go through it and never get the beauty of the lesson, or the ability to help someone else through similar situations.

The diagnosis of a chronic illness is one of the main destruction points of a marriage, statistically 75% of these marriages end in divorce. We are obligated to share and help others know that a healthy marriage is still possible, if you're willing to be coached and mentored through the process. The mistake people make is trying to deal with all of it alone. No one is able to think past their own thoughts. We need someone else to look inside the boxes we've put ourselves in. We need them to tell us what's out there to aspire to, so that we can even realize there's a reason to cut away at the duck tape that's sealing it up. Then you must become receptive to the process, understand that it will get gritty, grimy, and even painful, but this is the tunnel to your light. You have to go through it to grow through it.

Every couple has their thing. What is yours? There may not be a health challenge, but maybe there's adultery, financial, or a spiritual warfare battle of another kind. We all have our crosses to bear. The way we handle them determines the outcome. We grew up and began to understand we had to look at life differently, and figure out how to grow through the lessons and the pain we'd experienced. I knew I had a choice. I could surrender to God and ask for help or I could keep doing things my way, which clearly were not working. I could not make a decision for my husband, but I could become responsible for me, and start the work.

I had to decide that I had to do what I could do to improve the state of our marriage. I knew I had to focus on me. I turned my focus on chiseling away at my heart and carving out a better version of me. I was so broken and callused; those deep wounds were taken out on my husband even when I didn't realize it. I knew it would not serve the purpose for me to focus on him and what he was or wasn't doing, when I finally came to realize a huge piece of that painful puzzle hinged on me.

Lessons, Choices, and Decisions

I would be absolutely remiss in not sharing what the lessons have been along the way. The tests we go through in life, serve absolutely no purpose if we do not learn from what we've been through. Here's the golden nugget for this chapter. No matter what life hands you, make sure you immediately recognize it as a test of your faith and your resolve. Then, shift your mind to searching for the lesson and the why. Sometimes you don't get to know the why, but what I know for sure is that marriages are constantly tested and if you don't learn, you'll find yourself facing some of the same things over and over. I don't know about you, but I would rather not have to revisit some of the storms we've been through.

We don't always get a say in what we're faced with, but we do get a say in how we respond. Here's the secret, practice. When faced with a new challenge, practice taking the high road. I was taught by one of my mentors that it does not at all matter who's right, what matters is that your integrity stays in tact. You have a certain measure of integrity to maintain with your husband as well. The idea seems to be that they just have to take us like we are, but that was not your thought when you wanted him to notice you in your dating days. Sharpen your sword by reading the Word; start with a few minutes a day, until it's your daily habit. Fill your cup with positive things, friends, and surroundings, so that you have something to give. Most of us wear out because we have nothing left to give, which only happens when you don't intentionally refill.

In Ephesians 5:33 we are told *"However, each one of you also must love his wife as he loves himself, and the wife must respect her husband."* If there is no respect, we are saying loudly and clearly to our husbands that we don't love them. This scripture is not a request or a question. It's a command from God. Therefore, it's nonnegotiable. There is a grand possibility that I was told about this scripture many years ago. Evidentially, I was not in a place to receive it because if so, I could have saved myself a lot of headache, and heartache trying to figure out how to love my husband. I kept asking him what he needed. He couldn't articulate it. As a woman, of course, I didn't understand not being able to express yourself. So this left me spinning my wheels and trying to do what I thought I was supposed to do with no direction, no roadmap, just my own thoughts. I definitely did not understand that life's blueprint is between the front and back covers of my Bible.

Before you say I do, take time to know you. Do your work to be whole and bring 100% of yourself to the marriage and be ready to receive 100% from your spouse. Seek God's Word and read what it says about you and your role in marriage. Do not expect back what you are not prepared to give.

I answered the call to speak as a married woman, so that other wives could be blessed by our story, and get an understanding to know they are not alone. We are in control of our decisions, our actions, and our responses. Take time to choose wisely, as every action has a reaction, adverse or positive. Again, it's a choice. We get to make the decision to rise up, or fall into the enemy's plan. He does not want marriages to survive and pushes hard against them to succeed because then he can destroy the whole family. Be your husband's rib through the good, the bad, the ugly, the beautiful, the peaceful, the storms the ups and downs. Unstated expectations kill marriages. What's not said can't be expected. Have frequent check-ins with your spouse; as we grow, change, and evolve so will your marriage. If you don't come together with your common goal, you will likely go two different directions. Our marriages need goals just as our personal lives do. Don't leave your futures to chance. Be intentional.

No More Do Overs

Timeko Whitaker
Managing Editor

Joining the Army at the tender age of 17 gave me a fresh start and sort of a do over where no one knew anything about me or my past. I could literally create and become who I wanted to be. Leaving Waterloo, Iowa in my past meant so many things to me, like leaving my silent abuser behind as well as the ex-boyfriend who threatened to kill both me and my mother. It meant leaving behind the feelings of insufficiency and insignificance. It meant leaving behind the childhood bullies and battles I silently fought. It meant leaving behind the girl with low self-esteem and a speech impediment who was there but never quite fit in with the crowd. I was now an independent young lady. I quickly became self-sufficient, in need of no one. I didn't have to concern myself with fitting in any longer because army girls were welcome to every party. I gained a confidence giving me an opportunity to grow immensely and quickly. Every challenge I conquered made me stronger, surefire and ready for the next. The more demanding the better. Within a few short years I advanced from barely making it through basic training to repelling out of helicopters and graduating from Air Assault School. I remember it like it was yesterday. Standing proud as one of five females remaining on graduation day. Huoooah! The fact that I had someone special in my life made it even richer. He enjoyed being with me and made me feel like I was the top pick of the military post. He was absolutely proud to have me on his arm. He wore me like a prized possession. I'd taken him home to meet the family and had been to his home town to meet his.

We'd been together for over a year when I started seeing familiar behavior patterns that resembled that which I had experienced in my past. It was like the jealousy and control came out of nowhere. He couldn't stand to be without me and was unhappy anytime a fraction of my day excluded him. It got pretty bad and the next thing I knew he was in custody of the military police, and I was on a flight to Korea for a new assignment. It was time for yet another do over in a new place with new people.

I was rising through the ranks quickly, doing well at my job and considered an up and coming success. However, this new place and different person reared the same result...another failed relationship. It had become my new normal. It happened a couple more times. Until this happened...

HE FOUND ME

"He who finds a wife finds a good thing" (Proverbs 18:22 NKJV)

When I made it to my next assignment it was different because I was different. I had experienced enough broken relationships and partied until I was no longer interested in that lifestyle. I knew I was ready to settle down but had no idea if, when, or how it would happen. I hadn't been the best judge of character and no longer trusted what I thought was best for me. Little did I know that was the best place to be. That's when my life completely changed. I wasn't looking, I was just living. Out of nowhere came this handsome, funny, down to earth, loving, kind, good ol' southern boy from Alabama named Eric. He pursued me until I finally agreed to a date. I knew instantly he was unlike any guy I've dated in the past. It felt so pure and so right. By this time I had gotten to the point where it was a requirement that my next relationship was with a man who truly loved the Lord. Although I wasn't super mature in the word of God, I had enough sense to know that if he loved the Lord, he would be capable of loving me.

"Husbands, love your wives, just as Christ loved the church and gave himself up for her." (Ephesians 5:25 NIV)

I knew the chances were slim that he would even consider abusing me mentally, physically, sexually or emotionally.

Eric was the kind of guy you could just grab a snuggly blanket and cuddle with, no worries of disrespect, dishonor or harm. He was the kind of guy you trust immediately. The feeling of safety that overcame me when he entered my life was indescribable. I knew it was the Lord answering my prayer when he shared with me that he was dedicating his life to the Lord and scheduled to get baptized the Sunday following our first date. Although he often drew the attention of women, his outward appearance was over shadowed by his inward glow that was both attractive and inviting. So what did I do? I fell in love and married him.

I SAID I DO TO WHAT I KNEW

Family came from near and far to celebrate our union. The wedding was great, reception was awesome, but within about a year it got real. I mean really real. We found ourselves angry, not speaking and second guessing our decision to become one. We were at divorce court's door, not knocking but about to break it down. He couldn't stand the sight nor thought of me and all I wanted was another do over.

What did I say "yes" to? This is not what I was expecting. Wait...I made a mistake I thought to myself often. After the initial shock and reality of what the commitment entailed, I had to make a decision on whether to leave or to settle into my new role as both wife and mother.

DO I EVEN KNOW HOW TO DO THIS?

It was then that I realized I'd never witnessed a strong marriage up close. I said I do to what I knew. The real question is what did I know? Was it the television shows that made marriage look so appealing, my grandparents' examples, or was it my distant aunts and uncles that I saw yearly at the family reunions with picture perfect marriages? I'm sure they had their own personal struggles, but my mom did a great job of ensuring a child always stayed in a child's place. If there were issues, I never knew. What and who shaped my perception of what this was supposed to be? Remember, I told you I was not super mature in the faith, so at that point it certainly wasn't biblical guidance. There I was trying to be a wife and had no clue what to do nor how to do it. That was so unfair to him.

My husband on the other hand, grew up in a home with both parents and had the luxury of watching how they communicated, handled disagreements, and disappointment. He witnessed how they both displayed love, compassion, and commitment. He observed as they modeled the sacrifice, celebrations, and self-less service. This is not to say that he saw the perfect example but he was able to have a true point of reference.

I said I do to what I knew. What I knew was that I was tired of being in abusive relationships, I wanted a best friend and lover, to have someone that I could love and laugh with, someone to celebrate and grow with, to share my fears, insecurities and struggles with, support and protect me, someone to father my children and to grow old with. I wanted to get married. That's literally all I knew.

I didn't know the true sacrifice it would take. In case you didn't notice, what I knew was a lot of what I wanted for me. I hadn't for a moment thought about what I would need to give up for us.

ME, ME, ME, ME, ME, ME, ME, MEEEEEEEE... (Clears throat)

Yep... like tuning up to sing, I quickly realized that's where I resided. In the tune of ME. The path from fairytales dreams to brokenness and then success led me to that place. Take care of me first. Somewhere deep on the inside I was determined not to be hurt again, not be taken advantage of and to remain on top of everything. I knew what I wanted and that's all that mattered. I was carefully guarded and protective in places I didn't even know existed. That made submitting to someone else even more challenging and unfamiliar. When I really read the passage *"Wives, submit yourselves to your own husbands as unto the Lord" (Ephesians 5:22 NIV),* I again began to question my decision. Submit? What does even mean?

It meant I could no longer do what I wanted to do when I wanted to do it. It meant I would have to put my marriage first even before my career, ambitions, and dreams. It meant I would have to learn how to communicate effectively. It meant I could no longer take the lead as I had been accustomed to doing. It meant hard work and a lot of intentionality. It meant no more relational do overs. More than anything else, it meant I would need to learn to submit unto the Lord in order to truly submit to my husband according to God's plan. I had to deal with me. There was no question of if I could because God's word told me in Phillippians 4:13 that I can do all things through him who gives me strength. However, because of free will, I had to answer the real question…Do I really want to become one and give up having and doing things my way?

YOKING OR CHOKING?

"Be ye not unequally yoked together with unbelievers." (2 Cor 6:14 NKJV) Through my research I've found that a yoke is a wooden bar or beam that joins oxen or other animals to work together in pairs. In the spiritual context Apostle Paul is speaking in reference to believers being yoked or joined together with unbelievers. I totally understand what Apostle Paul is conveying in this area. My personal belief and experience is that a man is unable to properly love a woman the way she is to be loved without first accepting Christ as his personal savior which binds him by the word of God. *"Husbands, love your wives, just as Christ loved the church and gave himself up for her."* (Ephesians 5:25 NIV)

I am amazingly blessed that my husband has shown this type of love for me over and over again. What did I do to deserve this type of man? The answer is nothing. It's a benefit of being yoked with a man who is a believer.

PAUSE POINT:
If you are a woman who is a believer of Christ, reading this and not yet married, please strongly consider ensuring the man you stand at the altar with is one who loves the Lord, and not only says it but shows it through his actions. Then and only then will he have the power (Holy

Spirit) to give himself up for you. By the way, just because he goes to church doesn't mean he's a believer.

Although my husband is a believer, I can imagine there has been plenty of times he wanted to walk out on me and our family, but God. In the same way there were times I wanted to walk away, but God! Without God's word and spirit we are left to our own fleshly, carnal desires that snatch us out of the God ordained family unit that he has instituted and into a selfish, sea of deceit and divorce. Selfishly we're left to make life changing decisions that impact everyone and everything around us. The impact divorce has on children is life long and can often be detrimental to their choices, lifestyles, and beliefs. I'm not saying being equally yoked would make everything perfect. However, it is my testimony that because we are both bound by the loving yet correcting word that's ordained by our heavenly father, we strategically move from feelings into faith and favor.

Again, the word "yoked" means bringing two together to work in pairs. When animals such as oxen, are yoked together unequally, they are unproductive and constantly going around in circles and could even be choked. In marital comparison, the most unfulfilled marriages consist of two people who are unbalanced and unproductive. They are headed in different directions and are choking the purpose out of one another. How can two walk together unless they agree? They find life happening but are experiencing great frustration with one another and are getting nowhere.

Can you imagine the pulling that goes on consistently in unequally yoked marriages? One wants to speed up while the other is trying to slow down. One wants to go in one direction and the other wants to go in the other. Unbalanced and unchecked, this can truly lead to a road of destruction and divorce. Unfortunately, this manifests more often in seasoned marriages. This often happens later in life when the honeymoon phase is over; the little kiddos are no longer the focus of attention and individually they're left to determine what has become of their lives. They begin to look for a way of escape from their current situation to embrace a newness that will provide a perceived win but is often a true loss.

Being equally yoked in goals and desired lifestyles it very important to determine early in the relationship. It can be difficult to think 25years down the road and effectively communicate where you see yourself. Although difficult, it's still very necessary. Failure to deem this important can bring about detrimental results both emotional and relational.

Is it possible that this can be alleviated by communication and honesty early in the relationship?

PAUSE POINT:
My charge to those of you who are single and waiting to get married is to work diligently to determine your ideal future. Even if it's just a thought of where you would like to be. Communicate it effectively, let it be known and be true to it because even if you bury it in the present, it'll resurrect in your future. Make it a priority and requirement that you know first for yourself and then ensure you and your potential husband are both able to share where you see yourselves in the future. If one desires to work assiduously to reach goals and live a fast-paced life and the other desires a more simplistic life style, this can be a challenge no matter how much you both love the Lord. I said challenge, not impossible.

If you are waiting to be found, consider the following...
- Explore your likes and dislike
- Identify your non-negotiables
- Take time to learn and love yourself
- Identify your strengths and weaknesses
- Where do you see yourself in the future?
- What path will you need to take to get there?
- Settle in yourself before you settle in a marriage
- Make it a priority to learn how to be intimate with God
- Determine what type of person will be best suited to compliment your journey

IN IT TO WIN IT

"Therefore what God has joined together, let no one separate." (Mark 10:9 NIV)

When divorce was on the table for us it was always an option. It was a just in case to fall back on. It continued to be a thought and sometimes seemed to be a good idea. It lingered in the back of our minds and came to the forefront every time challenges occurred. It was only when we took it completely off the table that we fully put effort in for the win. Personally, it was only when I said "No more do overs" that I was totally committed to the win. When we closed the door to divorce, we immediately opened the door to allow the Holy Spirit to come in to guide us. The Holy Spirit shared with us beautiful fruit.

"But the fruit of the Spirit is love, joy, peace, forbearance, kindness, goodness, and faithfulness." (Galatians 5:22 NIV)

This is why Paul admonishes the importance of not being unequally yoked with unbelievers. Because we had the commonality of the Holy Spirit, there was an anointing of agreement that superseded every indifference, challenge, and attack against our marriage. We were able to stop fighting each other and began fighting for our family and our future. The more we fought together the stronger our marriage became. Before we knew it, we lost focus on everything that tried to separate us and gained joy in what we built together with the leading of the Holy Spirit.

Our marriage is not perfect. However, we are living fulfilled lives. We have committed to the process and God's plan for our family. Single ladies…hang in there. You are beautiful and your value is priceless. There is someone who will see your worth and will love you as Christ loves the church. Begin praying even now for your future husband. Married ladies… We wear many hats and hold many positions. Our positions can and will be filled by others as we transition roles in life, but you are the only one out of 7.6 billion people in the world that is anointed to be your husband's wife. Do it and do it well. Be in it to win it. No More Do Overs!

$\mathcal{A}$UTHOR CONTACT PAGE

Beatrice Beverly
Chapter Title: When Me, MySELF and I Turn Into US
Blessedx4ever2.wixsite.com/website
www.stoptheviolenceindy.org

Yalonda Brown
Chapter Title: B.R.O.K.E.N Through The Fight of My Life
justsayitllc2@gmail.com

Kiahna Davis
Chapter Title: Who Wears the Pants?
info@sacredandstunning.com
www.sacredandstunning.com

Cheryl Dixon
Chapter Title: The Journey of Our Life
Cdblessed2018@gmail

Myasha "Mya" Smith-Edmonds
Chapter Title: Mastering Marriage
info@myaspeaks.com
www.myaspeaks.com

Renee Flowers
Chapter Title: Intentional Love
ilyslove6@gmail.com

Lena Middleton
Chapter Title: There I Sat
pastorlenamiddleton@gmail.com

Chandra Orr
Chapter Title: Love Growth
Progress@Live4aLivin.org
www.Live4Livin.org

Tracy T. Pruitt
Chapter Title: The Battle Was Not Ours but We Won the War
tracypruitt23@gmail.com

Tisha Reid
Chapter Title: Open Your Gift and Reclaim Your Voice
Powerpoints4living@gmail.com

Sally Thompson
Chapter Title: Seeking To Be Made Whole Before Marriage
sallythompsonspeaks@gmail.com

Adrienne Wharton
Chapter Title: "Worthy to Be Loved...I Love My Hubby"
iluvmyhubbby100@gmail.com
www.iluvmyhubby.com

Renee Wharton
Chapter Title: Safe In His Arms
protectedheartwomensministry@gmail.com

LaTasha White
Chapter Title: Are You His Rib or Just the Scar?
www.johncmaxwellgroup.com/latashawhite/
latashawhite@johnmaxwellgroup.com

Timeko Whitaker
Chapter Title: No More Do Overs
www.authenticinstitute.com
authenticidentity@gmail.com

AUTHORS ARE AVAILABLE FOR
SPEAKING TOURS, CONFERENCES & PANEL DISCUSSION

BACKGROUNDS CONSIST OF BUT ARE NOT LIMITED TO:

NURSES

TRAINERS

PASTORS

REALTORS

THERAPIST

PREACHERS

LIFE COACHES

ACCOUNTANTS

INTERCESSORS

PASTOR'S WIVES

BUSINESS OWNERS

LEADERSHIP TRAINERS

MOTIVATIONAL SPEAKERS

AND MORE!

CONTACT AUTHENTIC IDENTITY COACHING, LLC
FOR MORE BOOKING INFORMATION
AUTHENTICIDENTITY@GMAIL.COM ~ 317.710.9533

AUTHENTIC
IDENTITY
INSTITUTE

LIST OF SERVICES

COACHING

SEMINARS

KEYNOTE TALKS

CERTIFICATIONS
5D Life Coach Certification
Human Behavior Consultant Certification (DISC)

ASSESSMENTS
(DISC) Personality Assessment
Spiritual Gift Assessment

JOHN MAXWELL CURRICULUM
Leadership Training
Mastermind Groups
Speaking

AIC BOOK PUBLISHING PARTNERSHIP DIVISION

www.authenticinstitute.com

THREE-DAY INTENSIVE
5D COACHING CERTIFICATION

TRAINING TO BECOME A 5D AUTHENTICALLY ME CERTIFIED
COACH WILL BE CONDUCTED USING BOTH LIVE AND
WEBINAR FORMATS. THE TRAINING AREAS WILL INCLUDE:

HUMAN BEHAVIOR CONSULTANT CERTIFICATION
SUMMARY OF COACHING PROFESSION
5D SEMINAR TRAINING
FACILITATION/PRESENTER TRAINING

COACH TIMEKO
WHITAKER
FOUNDER/CEO

FOR MORE INFO VISIT: AUTHENTICINSTITUTE.COM